How Le Make It Happen

The Secrets, Science and Strategies of World Class Leadership

Martin Robert Hall

Copyright © 2017 Martin Robert Hall

All rights reserved, including the right to reproduce this book, or portions thereof in any form. No part of this text may be reproduced, transmitted, downloaded, decompiled, reverse engineered, or stored, in any form or introduced into any information storage and retrieval system, in any form or by any means, whether electronic or mechanical without the express written permission of the author.

ISBN: 978-0-244-90943-7

PublishNation
www.publishnation.co.uk

CONTENTS

About the Author

Introduction   1

Chapter One: What Are We Missing?   7

Chapter Two: Man in the Mirror   21

Chapter Three: A Mindset for Growth   29

Chapter Four: In the Eye of the Beholder   41

Chapter Five: Driving Forces   51

Chapter Six: Intrinsically Tuned   69

Chapter Seven: Stop Monkeying Around   79

Chapter Eight: Make It Happen   111

Closing Comments   124

Acknowledgements   125

Bibliography   126

About the Author

Martin Robert Hall is a leading authority in the field of performance psychology. He consults to top athletes, organisations and ambitious individuals helping them to consistently perform at the highest level.

Martin shares his insights into the world of high performance through his writing and high impact keynote presentations.

This book brings together his work over the last five years, sharing proven insights his clients have benefitted from and also bringing together new research and strategies to first be revealed here in this book.

Martin's ideas have worked for elite sports people, including players from the likes of Manchester United and Manchester City FC. They have also worked for many successful organisations in the business and corporate world. The beauty of the ideas contained in this book is they can be applied by anybody. The principles and methods are universal.

Martin comes from a sports science background, studying the key elements that contribute to elite performance in the world of sport. Following this he had a career in the business world, selling and training in retail environments, and noticed many similarities when it came to driving results.

There are many parallels between high performance in sport and business. This book is a study into these parallels and in particular - the lessons that can be learnt from studying world class leaders in both fields.

What are the secrets of world class leadership?

How do these leaders get people to achieve way beyond most people's expectations?

And what does science say about this?

You are about to find out.

Introduction

Often, when I give the keynote speech at a company conference, I like to ask all the leaders in the audience to give me a show of hands.

Invariably, about 10 percent of the hands in the room go up.

I then ask them how many hands I wanted to see go in the air, and they begin to see where I am going with my message.

If you were in that room, what would you have done?

Would you have raised your hand?

Would you have wanted to raise your hand?

Would you consider your job title before deciding whether to raise your hand?

A common misconception about leadership is that you must be in a position of authority to be classed as a leader.

Leadership is not a title. Leadership is a mindset.

Let me share an interesting study with you to exemplify my point.

In 1968, a lady called Kitty Genovese was murdered in the middle of a busy neighbourhood in New York. There were thirty-eight witnesses to the murder who stood by and did not step in to assist or even call the police.

Social psychologists Bibb Latané and John Darley became fascinated with the lack of response in this particular case and looked into the psychology of the cause. They popularised the concept of "the bystander effect". The bystander effect occurs when the presence of others discourages an individual from intervening in an emergency situation.

There has been lots of research done in this particular area since, not just from Latané and Darley.

Dr Robert Cialdini, a professor in psychology, talks about this particular problem in his book *Influence*.

In one experiment, college students in New York acted as though they were having epileptic seizures. When there was only one bystander present, the student received an offer of help 85 percent of the time. But when five bystanders were present, the student only received an offer of help 31 percent of the time.

Another study involved smoke coming from under a door. Seventy-five percent of the individuals who passed by reported the leak, but when the leaks were seen by three-person groups, the smoke was reported only 38 percent of the time.

What does this show, and what does it have to do with leadership?

It shows us that when people are in a group, they assume that somebody else will take the lead.

This phenomenon, therefore, can have a huge impact on team and organisational performance, when people are always looking around them for somebody else to take the lead, especially in times of crisis.

This is just one of the interesting ways in which we stop ourselves from taking the lead in situations.

We often talk ourselves out of doing things.

What is the price of this?

And if we do it in emergency situations as stark as the one above, then in how many other situations are we holding ourselves back?

In my study into the world of high performance and great leadership, I have noticed four types of people:

Those who make it happen.

Those who watch it happen.

Those who stop it happening.

And those who say what happened!

Leaders make it happen.

There are many lessons we can learn from great leaders to enhance our own lives and our leadership potential. This book is a look into the world of high performance and great leadership.

What do the best of the best do to influence extraordinary performance?

What does the world of psychology say about this?

What can we learn from scientific studies to enhance our own leadership potential?

How can we apply these lessons in our own lives?

This isn't just a book about positive thinking. Great leadership is about much more than that. Even the most positive and highly experienced leaders can fall victim to their own minds and the complexities of human behaviour.

Understanding the underlying psychology and science is key to navigating your way around the trapdoors that even the most well-intentioned leaders fall down from time to time.

Two nuggets.

There are two pieces of advice I have received in my life which have really made an impact on me.

The first is one is to always remain open-minded and curious. Don't dismiss something that you don't fully understand. The more curious and open-minded you are to new ideas and new ways of doing things, the further you will go. It is something I have witnessed in the best leaders: they are always learning. They are continually open to new ideas; they are always seeking the edge. It is this mindset which is central to them becoming great.

> *"Use only that which works and take it from any place you can find it."*
>
> ## Bruce Lee

I suspect you already adopt this approach in your life; otherwise, you wouldn't have picked up this book. However, a gentle reminder is always useful.

While you navigate your way through this book, keep an open mind to the ideas and insights I am going to share with you. I'm not asking you to agree with everything inside, just to remain open and curious as to how it may apply to you, regardless of your current level of knowledge or mastery.

If you adopt this mindset, I promise you that you will get maximum value from what is inside.

The second piece of advice?

Always borrow money from pessimists; they don't expect it back!

Now, let's get serious. Get comfortable, and get ready to dive in. But just before you do…

How to read this book

I did not design this to be a wordy book. Let's face it, people's lives are busier than ever. This book is designed to make you think about the concepts inside and the best way to get the most value from it is to reflect on the ideas and questions it raises for you.

I encourage you to read it with a pen and paper and make notes. You will find blank pages at the end of each chapter to do so, with some accompanying questions at times to trigger the thinking process.

You may want to read it all the way through and then come back and reflect on each chapter individually. Alternatively you may plan reflection time at the end of each chapter as you go through. Either way, take the time to think.

It has been estimated that we only retain about 10 percent of what we read and approximately 90 percent of what we see, hear and put into practice. Reflection will help you put the ideas in this book in to action.

"The great aim of education is not knowledge but action"

Herbert Spencer

What Are We Missing?

"Reality is merely an illusion, albeit a very persistent one."

Albert Einstein

The human brain is an amazing machine. It has a remarkable ability to convince us that what we are experiencing is real and true. We are guided by our thoughts and impressions on a daily basis, and most of the time we trust them to navigate us through our busy lives, often acting automatically on intuition and impulse.

Much of the time, these intuitive thoughts and impulses turn out to be true, but not always.

We can often find ourselves feeling confident even when we are wrong. On the flip side, we can also find ourselves feeling doubtful when everything else would point in the direction of being on the right track.

As brilliant as our brains are, there are also many flaws and fallacies that can prevent us from reaching our potential.

Some are remarkably simple.

Imagine you are asked to watch a short video in which six people pass a basketball between them. Three of them are dressed in white shirts and three of them in black shirts. While you watch the video, you must keep count of the number of passes made by the people in white shirts.

At some point, somebody dressed in a gorilla suit strolls into the middle of all the action, faces the camera, beats their chest, and then leaves after spending nine seconds on the screen.

Would you see the gorilla?

Most people intuitively respond to this question with "Of course I would."

How could something so obvious go completely unnoticed? you might think.

But when Christopher Chabris and Daniel Simons did this experiment at Harvard University in 1999, they found that half of the people who watched the video and counted the passes missed the gorilla. It was as though the gorilla was invisible.

What Chabris and Simons found most remarkable was that people find these results surprising. When the viewers were questioned about the gorilla, they were certain they would not miss such an event right in front of their very eyes.

The results of this experiment reveal two interesting lessons:
1. We miss a lot of what goes on around us.
2. We have no idea that we are missing it.

Psychologists called this effect "perceptual blindness".

If it is so easy to miss something as obvious as this, what else could we be missing?

How in control of our day-to-day decisions are we really?

How easily are we influenced?

What else is affecting our ability to make sound judgements and decisions?

In one classical study carried out by social psychologist John Bargh, students at New York University, notably between the ages of 18 and 22, were asked to assemble four-word sentences from a set of five words.

For one group of students, half the scrambled sentences used words that are often associated with the elderly, such as "forgetful", "wrinkle", and "grey".

Following this exercise, the students were then asked to walk down the hall to take part in another experiment. Unbeknown to the students, the short walk down the hall was being watched and timed. This was, in fact, the experiment. Bargh was measuring how long it took the young students to walk down the corridor, and found that the group who were exposed to the "elderly associated" words walked significantly slower than those who were not exposed to such words.

The response was termed "the Florida effect", and explains how our behaviour can be unconsciously influenced (or "primed", as the official term goes).

Predictably, when the students were questioned afterwards, none of the students were even aware of their change in behaviour after exposure to the words.

Several other interesting experiments have been designed to demonstrate the ease at which we are often influenced below our conscious awareness.

Melissa Bateson and her colleagues at Newcastle University carried out an experiment which is a great demonstration of the power of priming.

Staff in the office canteen were trusted to pay for their tea or coffee by putting money into an honesty box.

Each week, Melissa renewed the price list for tea and coffee in the canteen, although the prices remained the same. What changed was the picture at the top of the price list.

One week it would be a picture of flowers, and the next it would be of eyes from real faces.

Something remarkable happened.

During the weeks when the picture above the price list was of a pair of eyes, staff paid 2.76 times as much for their drinks as they did when the picture was of the flowers.

Of course, once again, nobody noticed while this was going on! The behaviour of the staff was being primed under their conscious awareness.

The studies on priming above really demonstrate the power our environment has on us and our behaviour.

Be careful of how you are priming people to perform with the environment you create.

Is the environment you are creating setting people up to succeed? Are you priming people to perform at a high level?

Throughout this book, we will look at ways to prime ourselves and others for high performance.

The power of our expectations.

What we expect to find, we very often do, whether it is good for us or not.

Taking charge of our expectations in any given situation, then, is a crucial element of high performance.

"What we see depends mainly on what we look for."

Sir John Lubbock

We see what we expect to see, not what is really there. Our perceptions prove this to us time and time again.

For example, would you think that pouring vinegar into your beer would help you to enjoy it that bit more?

I didn't think so!

But what if you didn't know it was vinegar?

Dan Ariely, Professor of Psychology at Duke University, gave study participants beer with balsamic vinegar in it without telling them, and when questioned, they favoured it over regular beer, while they hated it when they knew there was balsamic vinegar in it before they drank it.

Expectations change the actual experience we have. So we don't just imagine that beer with vinegar tastes bad, it actually does (but only if we know it's in the beer in advance).

How is that possible?

How can information change the physicality of our experience?

In one experiment Ariely talks about, participants were given a drink and told beforehand that it was their favourite brand. When they were told this information (compared with when they were not) the results of an MRI scan showed that more areas of the brain which light up when we experience pleasure became active, as well as those which are associated with higher level thinking and memory.

So the information we have about a certain experience beforehand is responsible for the quality of the actual experience to a large part.

What do you expect to get out of the situations you find yourself in most days?

Think of the number of situations you face every day and the expectations you have for those situations. Could you improve your expectations to enhance your experience?

I see an example of this whenever staff are sent on a workshop I am delivering.

There are people who are just happy for a day out of the office and, of course, most of the day passes them by as they joke around and enjoy the snacks and treats.

There are people who are frustrated about being out of the office because they have so much work on, and they fail to stay in the present and absorb the benefit too.

Finally, there are people who are excited to learn something new, and even if they just take one thing away, it may just be the difference that makes the difference and helps them to raise their game to another level or overcome a current challenge they are facing.

"Studies have shown that 90 percent of error in thinking is due to error in perception. If you can change your perception, you can change your emotion and this can lead to new ideas."

Edward de Bono

Take a look at the picture below.

Is it fair to say that the image of the man on the far right is larger than the image of the man on the far left?

The intuitive and immediate answer that springs to mind for most is yes. However, if you measure the size of all of the images, you will find they are the same size.

Superhuman thinking.

Many of us have often played the game where we imagine what superpower we would have if we had free choice. Heading the list is usually being invisible or being able to fly. The power to think is not one that would normally spring to mind.

Edward de Bono, the leading psychologist who originated the term "lateral thinking" in the 1960's, believes that our ability to think is the most important human skill, yet one which is too often neglected.

"Lateral thinking" is basically a technical way of saying "thinking outside the box". It is a way of looking at problems in a creative and unusual way and arriving at a new solution that wasn't obvious at first glance.

Humour is a form of lateral thinking.

An old man dies and goes to hell. When he gets there, he sees his friend, a 90-year-old man, with a beautiful woman sitting on his knee. He says to his friend, "This can't be hell—you're not being punished, you're having fun!"

His friend replies, "This is punishment-for her!"

Lateral Thinking

De Bono wrote extensively on how anyone can learn to think differently. One of the ways in which to do this is through practising with lateral thinking puzzles, problems, and riddles.

Take a look at the riddles below and see if you can solve them. Remember that you must try and think of creative ways to solve them. Think outside the box!

1. What is a five-letter word that becomes shorter when you add two letters to it?

2. A man marries twenty women but he still only has one wife. How is this possible?

3. A woman is pushed out of a small aeroplane without a parachute but survives with no injuries apart from a few bruises. How is this possible?

4. How can you throw a ball as hard as you can and make it stop and return to you without hitting anything and with nothing attached to it?

5. Four people try to get underneath one small umbrella. Somehow, everyone manages to stay completely dry. How is this possible?

6. There are three switches outside a windowless room connected to three light bulbs inside the room. How can you determine which switch is connected to which bulb if you are only allowed to enter the room once?

Answers to the riddles are at the end of the chapter.

Learning to look at things differently, to challenge our perceptions and the flaws in our thinking, is key to high performance. Being prepared to look at things in a different way leads us to new solutions and new ways of doing things, leaps in performance which otherwise wouldn't have occurred.

Challenging those around us to see things differently is the key to constant improvement. Otherwise, we will continue to do things the way they have always been done, and then we are in danger of being left behind.

All great advancements throughout history, leaps in science, technology, and innovation, are a result of thinking in a new way.

No idea is a stupid idea.

"No matter what people tell you, ideas and words can change the world."

Robin Williams

"Good morning, everyone, and welcome to Bisham Abbey." said Clive Woodward, newly appointed manager of the England Rugby team.

"For the next hour, we'll be talking and thinking about how England plays rugby. In the five weeks leading up to our autumn Internationals, we'll be doing quite a bit of talking during meetings before we even think of heading down to the pitch. You may think it unusual that rugby players should spend so much time in the meeting room. Let me try and explain why I think we need to do this at the moment.

"I believe there are currently five teams in the world who could win the World Cup in 1999, and we all know who they are. We all have roughly the same standard of players, the same equipment, and the same physical training routines. So what makes the difference between the winning team and the team that comes fifth? I believe the team that actually wins the World Cup will be the team that has the best mindset that encompasses new ideas and change."

Clive Woodward had made his entrance.

He talked about how, in order to become better, they needed to embrace change and be open to doing things differently.

With the advice of management consultant Humphrey Walters, he created a culture where no idea was regarded as a dumb idea. It might not be used, but they encouraged idea after idea and an environment where nobody would be ridiculed for suggesting something out of the ordinary.

As a result, one of the many creative ideas to be implemented was how they improved the changing rooms. The ground committee at Twickenham wouldn't direct any money to improve them even though Woodward had described them as looking like a prison cell. So they called up the TV programme *Real Rooms*, who jumped at the chance to spruce them up, and the result was incredibly successful.

Woodward kept it a secret for the players until they walked into the changing room before a game with rivals Wales to see individual cubicles with hand-carved English oak name placards for each player and the words "To Be the Best" plastered all over the walls.

This is just one of hundreds of ideas that came out of creating this fearless creative environment, meaning ideas could be thrown into the mix with no fear whatsoever of ridicule. In fact, it can be a very fun process when you know you are not going to be scorned, which in turn enhances creativity even further.

We didn't lose.

Vince Lombardi, arguably the greatest ever American football coach, understood the power of seeing things differently when it came to winning. He once summarised the performance of his team following a defeat, saying:

"We never lost the game, we just ran out of time."

Lombardi knew that the success of his team was an inside game first and foremost, and that begins with the way we think.

When we change the way we think, we change what we do.

This is the starting point for how all great leaders **make it happen**.

> *"When we change the way we look at things, the things we look at change."*
>
> Dr Wayne Dyer

In the poem on the next page, the author Portia Nelson was describing her life story in five stages and it captures beautifully how we can often navigate ourselves through change.

There's a Hole in My Sidewalk

I walk down the street.
There is a deep hole in the sidewalk
I fall in.
I am lost…I am helpless.
It isn't my fault.
It takes forever to find a way out.

I walk down the same street.
There is a deep hole in the sidewalk.
I pretend I don't see it.
I fall in again.
I can't believe I am in the same place.
But, it isn't my fault.
It still takes me a long time to get out.

I walk down the same street.
There is a deep hole in the sidewalk.
I see it is there.
I still fall in…it's a habit.
My eyes are open.
I know where I am.
It is my fault. I get out immediately.

I walk down the same street.
There is a deep hole in the sidewalk.
I walk around it.

I walk down another street.

Answers to the lateral thinking riddles:

1. The word "short" becomes "shorter" when you add two letters.
2. The man is a priest and is marrying the women to other people, not to himself.
3. The aeroplane was standing still on the ground when the woman was pushed out.
4. You go outside and throw the ball upwards into the air.
5. It wasn't raining while the people tried getting under the umbrella.
6. Switch on the first switch, leave it on for a minute, and then switch it off again. Then switch on the second switch and enter the room. The second switch will be connected to the light that is on, the first switch will be connected to the light with the warm bulb, and the third switch will be connected to the light with the cold bulb.

Man in the Mirror

"Be the change you wish to see in the world."

Mahatma Gandhi

Being somebody who makes it happen is about being the inspirational example.

This means we must start with ourselves.

In 1996, Jim Collins and his team set out to answer a simple question: can a good company become a *great* company? And, if so, how?

They embarked on a five-year study to figure out the answers to this one question. They selected eleven companies whose stock had skyrocketed in comparison with other companies in their industry. These eleven companies had to show sustained performance, maintaining this leap to "great" for at least fifteen years.

They discovered some core fundamentals that were responsible for the leap from good to great, but perhaps the most interesting and important was the type of leader that lead the company into greatness.

What they found may surprise you. If you are imagining an imposing, mesmerising, larger than life character displaying egocentric qualities, then you would be wrong.

Collins coined the phrase "the antithesis of egocentric celebrity" to describe the type of leadership he discovered.

What did he mean by this?

Collins shares the example of Darwin Smith, who in 1971 became the chief executive of Kimberley Clark. He inherited a company that for 100 years had been merely good, never great. In the twenty years since Smith took charge, he took the company from performing way below the general stock market to outperforming the general stock market by over four times, leaping ahead of the likes of Coca-Cola, General Electric and Hewlett Packard.

Smith was a shy and reserved man, shunning any attempt at the spotlight. He didn't show any of the swagger you might expect from somebody who led such a turnaround in results.

So what did they find? What type of leader was Darwin Smith?

Collins tells of a time when, early in Smith's tenure as chief executive, a director pulled him aside to remind him that he lacked the qualifications for the position. Smith was later quoted summarising his tenure by saying, "I never stopped trying to become qualified for the job."

Smith may not have been a charismatic leader who oozed self-confidence. However, he was far from weak. He made the decisions that were required when he needed to. Smith had the resolve to overcome all the challenges he faced, to persist in the face of difficulty, and to lead his company to greatness.

Collins and his team found similar leadership in all of the eleven companies that went from good to great. They termed this "Level 5 leadership": "A paradoxical blend of personal humility and professional will."

This type of leader somewhat deflects the adulation whilst displaying a steel resolve to do whatever it takes to make a company great. It isn't as though they have no ego or self-interest—they are incredibly ambitious people—but their ambition is first and foremost for the organisation and its greatness, not for themselves.

"The antithesis of egocentric celebrity"—it was less about them and more about us. "We", not "me".

Another leader to display similar qualities in the world of sport, whom I have admired for many years, is Sir Alex Ferguson. When in charge of Manchester United Football Club, you would regularly hear him talk about "Manchester United" and not himself. He always mentioned the club first and foremost, and the standards he set were driven not just by himself but by what he regarded as the standards and values that grew from the traditions and values of the club. Even if it was his relentless drive that instilled these values in all of his players and staff, he never claimed them as the "Alex Ferguson" way.

Never stop trying to become qualified.

Note the words above: "a paradoxical blend of personal humility and professional will". "Paradoxical" because we wouldn't necessarily put those two words together.

What does that mean, and what can we learn from it?

The word humility comes from the Latin word *humilis*, which means low. Lowering one's sense of self-importance, you might say.

This is the opposite of the egocentric and often arrogant qualities we frequently witness from people who achieve extraordinary feats.

Be sure not to mistake this for a lack of confidence or courage, however.

Lowering our own self-importance opens us up to continuous improvement. It is the opposite of the "I know it all" mentality which prevents people from improving themselves.

Inspirational leaders look in the mirror, not out of the window.

They look to themselves to improve first. They take responsibility.

They are humble enough to do so. They are not scared to show their vulnerability. It takes courage to not know all the answers and to be open about it.

They are not trying to impress and prove they are better than others.

David Rockefeller, the leader of Chase Manhattan Bank in the 1960's, was known as a dominant, controlling leader. His managers reportedly lived in day-to-day fear of his disapproval. They used to feel relief at the end of each working day if they managed to get through it without being scorned. Even long past his heyday, senior managers refused to suggest new ideas because they were too worried about being ridiculed and made to feel small.

In the study of companies that went from good to great, Collins found something very interesting in the companies who never actually reached "great". He found in these companies that the leader became one of the main things that people worried about.

When leaders become too controlling and feared, they keep people from learning, growing, and moving forward. The cumulative effect of this on a company or team performance can be incredibly limiting.

When Jack Welch took over General Electric in 1981, the company was valued at 14 billion dollars. Twenty years later, the company was the most valuable company in the world, valued at 490 billion dollars.

Jack Welch was one of the most revered and successful CEOs in the world. Known for his fierce passion for winning and love for people, Welch was a humble leader.

He would regularly engage with his frontline employees to find out what was going on at the ground level in his business. General Electric has hundreds of thousands of employees, so you can imagine what a busy and important person Welch was. It would have been easy for him to get caught up in his own sense of self-importance, yet he didn't, and he stayed engaged in what was going on right down to the ground level of the business. He was interested in people. He was humble enough to listen to all the people in his organisation, and he regularly did so.

It wasn't his title that made him a leader.

Welch was a one-off, you might think?

He was born that way?

He was lucky; one of the fortunate few?

In fact, by Welch's own admission, he was far too full of himself early in his career. He was described as arrogant, as somebody who couldn't take criticism and wasn't willing to work hard enough on himself.

In his autobiography *Straight from the Gut* there is a whole chapter dedicated to the times when he was too full of himself! He tells of a time when he thought he could do no wrong and he acquired three companies which led to GE losing hundreds of millions of dollars.

Jack learnt that there is a fine line between self-confidence and excessive pride.

In his own words, "Arrogance is a killer and wearing ambition on one's sleeve can have the same effect. There is a fine line between arrogance and self-confidence. Legitimate self-confidence is a winner. The true test of self-confidence is the courage to be open, to welcome change and new ideas regardless of their source."

The Guy in the Glass

by Dale Wimbrow, (c) 1934

When you get what you want in your struggle for pelf,
And the world makes you King for a day,
Then go to the mirror and look at yourself,
And see what that guy has to say.

For it isn't your Father, or Mother, or Wife,
Who judgement upon you must pass.
The feller whose verdict counts most in your life
Is the guy staring back from the glass.

He's the feller to please, never mind all the rest,
For he's with you clear up to the end,
And you've passed your most dangerous, difficult test
If the guy in the glass is your friend.

You may be like Jack Horner and "chisel" a plum,
And think you're a wonderful guy,
But the man in the glass says you're only a bum
If you can't look him straight in the eye.

You can fool the whole world down the pathway of years,

And get pats on the back as you pass,

But your final reward will be heartaches and tears

If you've cheated the guy in the glass.

A Mindset for Growth

"I have not failed. I've just found 10,000 ways that won't work."

Thomas Edison

Did you know that Steve Jobs was fired from Apple in the earlier years?

Did you know that the world's greatest basketball player, Michael Jordan, failed to make his high school basketball team?

Did you know that the famous scientist Albert Einstein could not speak fluently until the age of nine?

Did you know that Steven Spielberg, one of the most influential filmmakers of all time, had such poor grades in high school that he failed to get into university?

Did you know that The Beatles, widely viewed as the most successful band of all time, were rejected numerous times before they got signed by a record label?

You can probably see where I am going with this.

Failure is not final. Clearly.

A clear pattern emerges when you study some of the greatest performers the world has ever seen. Failure is a constant, but never is it an excuse.

Stanford psychologist Carol Dweck has done some fascinating research into the power of our beliefs and the effect they have on our overall happiness and success.

In her research, Dweck and her colleagues found that one of the most powerful beliefs we carry about ourselves is the view we hold about our own ability and intelligence.

Is it fixed, or can it be developed?

Are some of us more genetically gifted than others?

Are we limited in our abilities, or can we improve at anything?

Dweck discovered that there are two meanings when it comes to ability—a fixed ability that needs to be proved, and a changeable ability than can be developed through learning.

From this discovery, she coined the terms "fixed mindset" and "growth mindset".

Dweck states that when we enter either one of these mindsets, we enter a new world. In one world—the world of fixed traits—success is about proving yourself. Proving you are smart or talented. Validating yourself. In the other—the world of changing qualities—it's about stretching and developing yourself, and learning new things.

In the fixed world, failure is about a poor result. Losing. Being rejected. Losing your job. Being demoted. Looking stupid.

In the growth world, failure is about not continuing to learn and grow. Not seeking out new challenges. Not fulfilling your potential and setting yourself new goals.

People in the fixed world have a very black and white view on situations.

"Believing that your qualities are carved in stone creates an urgency to prove yourself over and over. If you have only a certain amount of intelligence, a certain personality, and a certain moral character—well, then you'd better prove that you have a healthy dose of them. It simply wouldn't do to look or feel deficient in these most basic characteristics.

"I've seen so many people with this one consuming goal of proving themselves—in the classroom, in their careers, and in their relationships. Every situation calls for a confirmation of their intelligence, personality, or character. Every situation is evaluated: Will I succeed or fail? Will I look smart or dumb? Will I be accepted or rejected? Will I feel like a winner or a loser?"

One of the reasons the growth mindset is so appealing and effective is that it creates a passion for learning rather than a hunger for approval.

Qualities such as intelligence and creativity can be cultivated through effort and deliberate practice, states Dweck. She also states that qualities such as leadership, love, and friendship can be developed through having the same growth mindset.

People with the growth mindset are not discouraged by failure because they don't see themselves as failing in those situations, they see themselves as learning. It's all part of the process. Failure isn't final.

Does this mindset ring any bells? Can you see a similar pattern in the people that I opened this chapter with?

"Why waste time proving over and over how great you are, when you could be getting better? Why hide deficiencies instead of overcoming them? Why look for friends or partners who will just shore up your self-esteem instead of ones who will also challenge you to grow? And why seek out the tried and true, instead of experiences that will stretch you? The passion for stretching yourself and sticking to it, even (or especially) when it's not going well, is the hallmark of the growth mindset. This is the mindset that allows people to thrive during some of the most challenging times in their lives."

Carol Dweck

The paradox of effort.

Most people will recognise that nothing can be achieved without effort.

But the paradox of effort is that it robs you of your excuses. Once you have really tried, you can no longer say, "I could have been."

This is too hard for people who live in the fixed world to take, because once they land on this realisation, there is no way out. Failure is final.

In the fixed world, everything is driven by your outcomes. If you fail, or if you are not the best, then it has all been a waste of time.

But in the growth world, people value what they are doing regardless of the outcome. As long as they are growing, learning, and challenging themselves, they are winning.

One of the great myths the growth mindset dispels is the need for confidence.

You don't need to be confident to become great at something. You can still plough into something with hard work and persistence, refusing to give up.

Let me repeat that because I think it is really important. **You don't need to be confident to become great at something.**

It seems that all great achievers adopt a similar mindset.

One of the athletes I refer to a lot in my work is Muhammad Ali. A highly skilled competitor, of course, but the main reason I frequently refer to him is for the mindset he adopted.

Ali was not a natural by any means. Not by the definition of "natural" that boxing experts held back then, anyway. He was too small; he didn't have the strength needed, nor the technique. He didn't move properly, his defence was poor, he was easy to hit, and his movement was all wrong.

On the other hand, Sonny Liston had all the characteristics of a natural. He was big, powerful, and he had the textbook moves. In the eyes of the experts (and the public) there was no way Muhammad Ali could beat Sonny Liston.

Liston was the most intimidating fighter of his day. He was classed by many as one of the best heavyweight boxers the world had ever seen. Many boxers were too scared to face Liston, including the British champion Henry Cooper, who said he would face Ali if he won but he wasn't willing to face Liston.

On 25 February 1965, Muhammad Ali (then known as Cassius Clay) won the World Heavyweight Championship against Sonny Liston, with Liston retiring at the start of the seventh round.

How did he do it?

What made Ali great was his mind. He understood the power of his psychology like all great achievers.

"Champions are made from something they have deep inside them—a desire, a dream, a vision. They have to have last-minute stamina, they have to be a little faster, they have to have the skill and the will. But the will must be stronger than the skill."

Muhammad Ali

Listen to how Ali did it in his own words: "I read everything I could where he had been interviewed. I talked with people who had been around him or talked with him. I would lay in bed and put all of the things together and think about them, and try to get a picture of how his mind worked."

Part of Ali's plan was to lower Liston into a false sense of security.

"Liston had to believe that I was crazy. That I was capable of doing anything. He couldn't see nothing to me at all but mouth and that's all I wanted him to see."

Instead of Muhammad Ali looking in the mirror and thinking he didn't have the physical attributes to be world champion and beat the likes of the talented powerhouse that was Sonny Liston, he found another way. He focused on developing the one thing he could control, and that was his mind. This was his key to greatness.

Love the struggle.

People who live in the growth world find enjoyment in the challenge. They welcome challenges, they show humility, and are always looking for ways to improve. They are not deterred by setbacks.

They realise failure isn't final, it's just a stepping stone on the road to success.

Somebody who epitomises this mindset is one of my clients. Her name is Carly Tait. In 2012, Carly found herself feeling incredibly inspired by the Olympic Games in London, just like I'm sure many other people did in the UK.

Following the Olympic Games, Carly found herself even more inspired by the Paralympic Games. The reason? Carly has a condition called cerebral palsy, which mainly affects her legs and her coordination. Carly was watching all of these incredible athletes who had various disabilities and wanted to go and experience it for herself.

Thinking this could be a once-in-a-lifetime opportunity, she convinced a friend to purchase a ticket with her (to the tune of several hundred pounds) and off they went, down to London, to watch the Paralympic Games.

At the time, Carly was 26 years old. She worked in marketing. She was a self-confessed party girl. She loved a night out, she hated exercise, and she smoked twenty cigarettes per day.

Don't get me wrong, though; Carly loved her life!

Once inside the Olympic Stadium, she fixed her eyes on these incredible athletes. Some of them had no arms. Some had no legs. Some of them were blind. Some of them had cerebral palsy.

Something struck her. She felt inspired by these people.

If they can do something like that, why can't I? she thought.

She told her friend and her friend just laughed and said "Carly, you smoke twenty fags a day and you hate sport!", reminding her why not!

Carly continued watching.

"I think I am going to give this a go," came the next comment from Carly. "I am going to give wheelchair racing a go."

Yeah, yeah, her friend must have thought.

You can only imagine her friend's face when Carly declared that in four years' time she was going to be heading to the next Paralympic Games in Rio de Janeiro!

Once they got back to Manchester, Carly sought out the clubs across the country where she could learn to wheelchair race. There were five wheelchair racing coaches in the country and, fortunately for Carly, one just down the road in Stockport, which is where she worked at the time.

So off she went one Tuesday evening to give it a go.

When she got there, she was too overweight to fit in the wheelchairs the athletes raced in. She was mortified, as you can imagine. But did it stop her?

The coach offered her a standard wheelchair to go around the track in, to get used to the technique.

Carly kept on returning to training, still undeterred. Eventually she got in the race wheelchair, and she improved each time.

When she got to the point where she was ready to start racing, she had a whole new experience.

She was confronted with the terrifying new feeling of pre-race nerves. If you have ever done anything new in front of an audience, you will know exactly how these nerves feel!

Did that stop her?

No. This was the point at which we started working together.

Carly improved and improved. Her times came down and down as she worked harder and harder.

She went to the European Championships in 2016 and won two silver medals. Following that, in the summer, she was selected to represent Great Britain at the Paralympic Games in Rio, realising her lofty (some might say) dream.

Can you see the same pattern that has emerged in this story? Refusing to give up at many points along the way helped Carly to achieve something incredible. It really is the stuff of dreams!

How much of your potential could you fulfil by adopting the growth mindset?

Can you see that there really are no limits? What are you telling yourself you cannot do?

What about the beliefs you have about those around you?

"Don't Quit"

When things go wrong, as they sometimes will,

When the road you're trudging seems all uphill,

When the funds are low and the debts are high,

And you want to smile, but you have to sigh,

When care is pressing you down a bit,

Rest, if you must, but don't you quit.

Life is queer with its twists and turns,

As every one of us sometimes learns,

And many a failure turns about,

When he might have won had he stuck it out;

Don't give up though the pace seems slow—

You may succeed with another blow.

Often the goal is nearer than

It seems to a faint and faltering man,

Often the struggler has given up,

When he might have captured the victor's cup,

And he learned too late when the night slipped down,

How close he was to the golden crown.

Success is failure turned inside out—

The silver tint of the clouds of doubt,

And you never can tell how close you are,

It may be near when it seems so far,

So stick to the fight when you're hardest hit—

It's when things seem worst that you mustn't quit.

Author Unknown.

In the Eye of the Beholder

"Some are born great, some achieve greatness, and some have greatness thrust upon them."

William Shakespeare

In 1968, the work of two psychologists, Robert Rosenthal and Lenore Jacobsen, studied the effects of tutor expectations on the performance of their students.

They took intelligence pre-tests with the children and then told teachers the names of 20 percent of them who were showing "unusual potential for intellectual growth", and predicted they would bloom with the academic year.

They then sat back and watched what was to unfold.

Unknown to the teachers, these children were randomly selected with no relation to the intelligence test. Eight months later, they re-tested the children, and the results showed that the randomly selected children, who the teachers thought would bloom, scored significantly higher.

They called this "the Pygmalion effect", named after the legendary figure of Cyprus. Pygmalion was a sculptor who carved a woman out of ivory. He fell in love with the woman in his statue and wished he would meet a woman just like her, which he did shortly after.

The results from this study (and there have been hundreds of studies done in this same area since) showed that positive expectations of others influence performance positively, and negative expectations do the opposite.

"When we expect certain behaviours of others, we are likely to act in ways that make the expected behaviour more likely to occur." (Rosenthal & Babad, 1985).

You may recall times in your life when this effect has taken place on you, if you had a teacher in a particular subject in school that believed in your abilities, or a boss who did the same, and you stepped up to meet their expectations of you.

Great leaders have the ability to see more in people than they can often see in themselves.

Steve Jobs is somebody who was famously known for pushing people beyond their limits to often achieve what was considered impossible. His colleagues dubbed this effect "reality distortion field" after an episode of *Star Trek* in which aliens create a convincing alternative reality through sheer mental force.

An early example of this was when Jobs was on the night shift at Atari and pushed Steve Wozniak to create a game called *Breakout*. Wozniak said it would take months, but Jobs stared at him and insisted he could do it in four days. Woz knew that was impossible, but he ended up doing it.

Those who had not worked for Jobs and didn't really understand him interpreted the reality distortion field as a euphemism for bullying and aggression. But those who worked with him admitted that the trait, as infuriating as it could be, led them to perform way beyond what they thought was possible.

Jobs and Apple had a fraction of the resources that Xerox or IBM had, yet Jobs acted as if the ordinary rules most people play by didn't apply to him, and he inspired his team to change the course of computer history as a result.

Debi Coleman, who was a member of the original Mac team, recalls, "It was a self-fulfilling distortion." Coleman won an award one year for being the employee who best stood up to Jobs. "You did the impossible because you didn't realize it was impossible."

One day, Jobs marched into the cubicle of Larry Kenyon, the engineer who was working on the Macintosh operating system, and complained that it was taking too long to boot up. Kenyon started to explain why reducing the boot-up time wasn't possible, but Jobs wasn't interested.

"If it would save a person's life, could you find a way to shave ten seconds off the boot time?" he asked. Kenyon conceded that he probably could. Jobs went to a whiteboard and showed that if five million people were using the Mac and it took ten seconds extra to turn it on every day, that added up to 300 million or so hours a year—the equivalent of at least 100 lifetimes a year.

A few weeks later, Kenyon had the machine booting up twenty-eight seconds faster.

The message is simple. Be careful what you expect from others and be careful what others expect from you. Have a look around and notice if it is having a positive or negative effect.

Inspiring others to perform at the highest level starts with ourselves.

We cannot force others to change but we can facilitate the change. Our very own expectations of others will have a direct impact on their behaviour, so checking in with ourselves and analysing our own perceptions of others is the starting point.

What expectations do you have of those around you?

Are your expectations having a positive impact or a limiting impact?

The examples above demonstrate the sheer influencing power of our own perceptions and the power of self-fulfilling prophecies.

A self-fulfilling prophecy is a prediction that directly or indirectly causes itself to become true by the very terms of the prophecy itself.

The placebo effect is an extremely powerful example of a self-fulfilling prophecy

Henry K. Beecher, a medic during World War Two, discovered the placebo effect while treating wounded soldiers. Henry ran out of the powerful painkiller morphine. In desperation, he continued telling the soldiers that he was giving them morphine, although he was actually infusing them with a water solution. Amazingly, 40 percent of the soldiers reported that the treatment reduced or erased their pain.

Modern day science helps us to better understand why those soldiers felt better. Beecher gave the soldiers a placebo—a substance that may look like a real medication, but isn't. One of the most common placebos that has been experimented with is a sugar pill, but they can take many forms including injections, procedures, devices, and even just a few encouraging words.

Much of the research on placebos is to do with the treatment of pain. Scientists have found that placebos can cause the brain to release pain-relieving chemicals. Research in this area shows that areas of the brain that process pain show reduced activity following placebo treatment.

One particular study in 2001 by Fernandez and colleagues showed that placebos can positively affect the symptoms of brain diseases. Parkinson's disease, a neurological condition marked by low levels of the brain chemical dopamine, is often treated with a dopamine drug called levodopa. Research has shown that placebos can increase the levels of dopamine in the brains of Parkinson's patients and help them move more easily, doing the same job that the drug levodopa is designed to do.

It seems that the placebo effect depends on a combination of factors such as verbal suggestion and the conditioning effects of our expectations.

How incredible that these expectations actually influence the chemicals our brain releases, which in turn can affect the pain or pleasure we experience within our body.

There have been numerous studies on the power of placebo since the original paper in 1955 by Henry K. Beecher, and they all demonstrate the power our beliefs can really have.

Are your beliefs setting you up for success or are they holding you back?

Over the course of our lifetime, we can unfortunately gather and collect many limiting beliefs that hold us back from achieving our potential.

We have already discovered how easy it is for us to be primed to think in a certain way, and the impact a few words can have on how quickly we walk. Well, the work of another psychologist, Martin Seligman, sheds even more light on the power our experiences can have on us if we are not careful and aware of what is going on.

In 1965, Seligman and his colleagues were doing research on classical conditioning, the process by which we associate one thing with another, for example sunshine and feeling good, or rain and feeling miserable!

Seligman conducted an experiment where he would ring a bell and give a light shock to a dog. After a while, the dog would react to the shock before it even happened. Seligman would only have to ring the bell for the dog to react like it had been shocked.

Seligman then discovered something interesting. He put each dog into a large crate that was divided down the middle with a fence low enough for the dog to see and jump over, should it need to.

The floor on one side of the fence was electrified, while on the other side it was not. Seligman then put the dog on the electrified side and administered a light shock. Expecting the dog to jump to the other side of the fence, he was shocked when the dog just lay down instead. It was as if the dogs had learned from the first experiment that there was nothing they could do to avoid the shocks, so they just gave up in the later part of the experiment.

Seligman described this condition as learned helplessness. Basically, not trying to help oneself out of a negative situation because the past has taught you that there is nothing you can do about it.

He later tried the second part of his experiment with dogs that had not been through the first part (classical conditioning) of the experiment. The dogs who had not previously been exposed to any shocks quickly jumped over the fence to escape the shocks, proving to Seligman that the dogs who lay down and acted helpless had actually learned that helplessness from the first part of the experiment.

What can we learn from this?

The way we view the negative events that happen in our lives has a big impact on how we react to those events and whether we feel helpless or not.

It is easy to be conditioned into certain ways of thinking, especially if we are not aware of it at the time.

Leaders create the conditions for themselves and others to overcome the negative effects of conditioning. They create an environment of high standards and positive expectations, and by doing so they help people to overcome phenomena like learned helplessness.

This is how leaders make it happen for themselves and for those around them.

Are you helping your people to see things differently?

Coaching them to change their own thinking and not just telling them?

Start by challenging your very own perceptions.

The Man Who Thinks He Can

By Walter D. Wintle

If you think you are beaten, you are;

If you think you dare not, you don't.

If you'd like to win, but you think you can't,

It is almost a certain- you won't.

If you think you'll lose, you're lost;

For out in this world we find

Success begins with a fellow's will

It's all in the state of mind.

If you think you're outclassed, you are;

You've got to think high to rise.

You've got to be sure of yourself before

You can ever win the prize.

Life's battles don't always go

To the stronger or faster man;

But sooner or later the man who wins is the one who thinks he can!

What has this chapter made you think about?

Are you aware of your own empowering and limiting perceptions and their impact?

Use the space below to make notes of any insights that come to mind.

Driving Forces

"Human behaviour flows from three main sources: desire, emotion and knowledge"

Plato

It is impossible to lead if you do not understand the innate human drives that are fundamental to motivation and behaviour.

Decades of research have provided us with numerous theories about what drives human behaviour. In this chapter, we will be taking a closer look at what these theories suggest and how we can use that to our advantage.

In the 1960's, Dr Paul Mclean, a leading neuroscientist, developed the famous triune brain theory for helping us to understand the brain in terms of how it has evolved over millions of years.

His theory proposes that there are in fact three brains in one, each of which has developed over successive years. These three brains do not operate independently of each other; there are numerous neurological pathways which connect each part of the brain, meaning they all influence each other.

Brain One

The reptilian brain. The oldest of the three brains. This part of the brain is responsible for our vital bodily functions such as heart rate, breathing, hunger, sexual drives, and our fight or flight system.

Its job is essentially to ensure that we survive and reproduce.

Brain Two

The limbic brain. Throughout evolution, as animals became more complex, this brain first emerged in mammals (sometimes referred to as the mammalian brain). Humans share this brain with the likes of dogs, cats, horses, and even mice. Their brains and this part of our brain are very similar, hence why many psychological studies have been conducted using these animals.

If you think about the difference between a lizard and a dog, or a snake and a horse, you will notice that dogs and horses have feelings like human beings. The limbic brain is responsible for our emotions and memory and is sometimes referred to as our emotional brain.

Brain Three

The neocortex. This part of the brain first existed in primates and is what separates humans from the rest of the animal kingdom. This part of the brain is responsible for the development of language, imagination, consciousness, and abstract thinking. The neocortex is flexible and has almost infinite learning capacity. It is sometimes referred to as the thinking brain or rational brain.

The battle of the brains.

For the sake of simplicity, I am going to focus on two areas of the brain as we further try and understand how these three parts of our brain drive our everyday behaviour.

These two I will refer to as "the emotional brain" and "the thinking brain".

This explains why often, we can have all the facts, reason, and logic to make a decision and still not make it because "it doesn't feel right."

These two parts of our brain are doing battle.

You will understand this battle if you ever been food shopping when you are hungry. Your thinking brain might be telling you all the healthy choices you must be making to stick to your new healthy eating plan, but your emotional brain is hungry and takes over, and we all know what happens next!

Human behaviour is largely driven by our limbic brain. As the maxim goes, "Reason leads to conclusion, emotion leads to action."

In the early 1990's, the neuroscientist Antonio Damasio made a ground-breaking discovery in decision making. He studied people with damage in the part of the brain where emotions are generated. He found that they seemed normal, except that they were not able to feel emotions. But they all had something peculiar in common: they couldn't make decisions. They could describe what they should be doing in logical terms, yet they found it very difficult to make even simple decisions, such as what to eat.

While our rational, thinking brain is conscious and knows what is going on, our emotional limbic system is working behind the scenes, meaning many of our decisions are based on emotion even if we are not aware of it.

The limbic system is carrying out our most important drives to keep us alive and safe. This is our priority, and therefore it is much more powerful than our thinking brain.

Think about going back thousands of years, when you may easily have been attacked by a tiger or a bear. When this happens, you have not got time to think about what to do! You need to act, not work out a plan. This part of the brain takes over and you run, or, if needed, you defend yourself (fight or flight).

So you can see, it makes sense that our limbic brain has such a powerful influence over our behaviour. Unfortunately, many of these natural drives we have are not suited to the modern world we live in.

This limbic system is responsible for keeping us safe and warning us when we are in danger of any sort. Now, when we perceive something dangerous, this system kicks in and often dumps a load of chemicals into our system that triggers the fight or flight response. This is how nerves work prior to an important event.

Our more rational, thinking brain might know that we are prepared, that there is no real threat to our health, but as much as we tell ourselves to stay calm, our limbic system is triggering emotions inside of us that make us want to get out of there as fast as we can.

You can now begin to see why sometimes we have such a hard time making decisions. This is why it is important for us to ensure that we engage both parts of our brain to drive high performance.

The thinking brain plays a crucial role in reigning in and controlling the urges of our deeper emotional brain. It helps us from exploding with anger when somebody upsets us, or lashing out when we feel like it, because we have learned from our social conditioning that this wouldn't be helpful to us in the long run.

It helps us to weigh up the risks in any situation based on our knowledge and experience, and not just on how we feel at the time. These two brains are communicating all the time and helping us to make decisions.

The thinking brain is acting a lot of the time like a controlling mechanism over our emotional side, which is why when we are tired and depleted we often have less willpower and can find ourselves irritated at smaller things. The more we ask our thinking brain to work, the less control it will have over our stronger emotional drives.

Several studies have shown that when somebody is challenged with a cognitive task, they are more likely to give in to temptations. One particular study gave participants a number to remember while they walked from one room to another. Everyone got numbers that varied in the number of digits, and remembering their number was the clear priority. When walking to the other room, they were interrupted and offered a reward for participating—a choice between chocolate cake and fruit. The evidence showed that the more digits people had to remember, the more likely they were to choose chocolate cake. The busier our thinking brain is, the less influence it has over controlling our emotional brain, which clearly has a sweet tooth!

Emotion wins over reason.

Human behaviour is not textbook. We like to think we are rational and often get confused when people behave irrationally, but a lot of things we do don't make rational sense. Let me give you another example.

Imagine somebody offers to give me ten pounds, but only if I share some of it with you. If you accept my offer of sharing it then we both get to keep the money, but if you reject my offer then neither of us gets to keep anything.

If I offered you six pounds, with me keeping four, would you take it? I imagine you would.

What if I offered you five, while I keep five? You would probably take that too.

But what if I offered you two pounds while I get to keep eight?

In studies done around the world on the same basis, most people rejected the final offer. This doesn't make any sense—not rationally, anyway. You would be two pounds richer and I would be eight pounds richer (both better off than before), and if you reject my offer then we both get nothing.

Of course, if our rational, thinking brain was in charge it would see this, but emotion takes over for most people. If you don't think it is fair, you will reject the offer even though your rational mind knows it makes no sense. Your desire for fairness (or your annoyance at my low offer) will override your rational mind, meaning you miss out.

In one study, researchers from the Harvard School of Public Health asked 257 students and staff which they would prefer:

Earning $50,000 a year when everyone else around them makes $25,000.

Earning $100,000 a year when everyone else around them makes $200,000.

Fifty percent chose the first option, leaving $50,000 on the table just to avoid earning less than their neighbours.

Again, emotional, not rational!

Two driving forces in people's lives.

The evidence is clear that two key driving forces in our life are emotion and reason, and engaging them both is key to driving high performance.

These driving forces have an enormous influence over the decisions we make, and our lives reflect the sum total of our decisions to date.

The best leaders don't just provide a sound argument or plan for achievement. They also get people highly engaged at an emotional level.

Somebody who captured the essence of this was Simon Sinek in his famous TED talk *Start With Why*.

In his talk, he gives the example of how Apple communicate to their customers, engaging them on an emotional level first and foremost.

Sinek presents the following three circles to demonstrate his message:

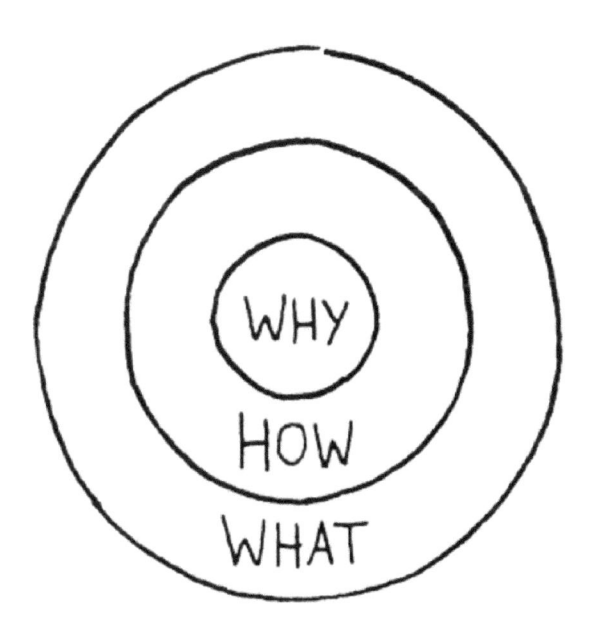

Apple is a good example because most people have heard of them, and most people get it. He says that unlike most companies, Apple communicate from the inside out, not the outside in.

He uses a simple marketing example to demonstrate his point. If Apple were like everyone else, then their marketing message would be something along the lines of:

"We make great computers. They are beautifully designed, simple to use, and user friendly. Want to buy one?"

He explains how this is the way most people communicate. We say what we do, we say how we are different or better, and then we expect some sort of behaviour in response, like a purchase or a vote or a decision of some sort.

"Here is our new law firm. We have the best lawyers and the biggest clients. We always perform for our clients—do business with us."

This is uninspiring, he says. It does not engage us on an emotional level.

This sort of communication only engages our rational thinking brain, and we now understand that this is not the dominant driving force in our decision making.

Sinek makes reference to the three levels of our brain in his presentation. He talks about the rational brain and how it is responsible for analytical thought and language. He also talks about the limbic brain and how this is responsible for our decision making and our behaviours. This has much more power over what we eventually decide to do.

The limbic brain is responsible for all of our feelings, like trust and loyalty. He argues that Apple communicates directly to this level of our brain, meaning we are more compelled to buy their products.

"When we communicate from the outside in, then yes, people can understand vast amounts of complicated information like features, benefits, facts, and figures - it just doesn't drive behaviour. When we communicate from the inside out, we are talking directly to the part of the brain that controls behaviour, and then we allow people to rationalize it with the tangible things we say and do. This is where gut decisions come from."

Apple communicate from the inside out. Instead of telling you what they do, they start by telling you why they do it. They simply reverse the order of the information.

"Here's how Apple actually communicates: everything we do, we believe in challenging the status quo, we believe in thinking differently. The way we challenge the status quo is by making our products beautifully designed, simple to use, and user friendly. We just happen to make great computers. Want to buy one?"

People don't buy what you do, they buy why you do it, Sinek says.

The original advert promoted by Apple narrated a poem called *The Crazy Ones*, featuring the likes of Einstein, Muhammad Ali, Martin Luther King, The Beatles, and Gandhi.

See the poem on the following page:

The Crazy Ones

Here's to the crazy ones.
The misfits.
The rebels.
The troublemakers.
The round pegs in the square holes.

The ones who see things differently.

They're not fond of rules.
And they have no respect for the status quo.

You can quote them, disagree with them,
glorify or vilify them.
About the only thing you can't do is ignore them.

Because they change things.

They push the human race forward.

While some may see them as the crazy ones,
we see genius.

Because the people who are crazy enough to think
they can change the world, are the ones who do.

Apple are engaging people at this deeper level of the emotional brain with this sort of communication, by appealing to your core beliefs and not just your rational thought of why you should buy a computer from them. They are appealing to something much deeper.

Engaging at the emotional level.

Sinek provides two further powerful examples of people being engaged at an emotional level.

The first is the story of the Wright brothers, who famously created the world's first ever successful aeroplane. While this is a well-known story, what isn't is the story about Samuel Pierpont Langley and his pursuit of powered manned flight at the same time.

Even though the Wright brothers are credited with being the first, early in the twentieth century, everybody was trying to create manned flight. The Wright brothers weren't alone.

Samuel Pierpont Langley had what many would assume the recipe for success and the best chances of being the first person to achieve manned flight. Langley was given 50,000 dollars by the War Department to figure out how to build the first aircraft. He had the money. He also had all the right connections; he held a seat at Harvard and knew all the smartest minds of the day, who he could call on for help and advice. Everything was in his favour. Even the New York Times were supporting his cause and followed him around rooting for him.

While all this was going on, a few hundred miles away in Ohio lived two brothers, Orville and Wilbur Wright. Unlike Langley, they had none of these favourable conditions which we would attribute to success. They had no money apart from the small proceeds they made from their bicycle shop. They didn't have anyone, not one single person on their team, who had a college education, and of course, they had zero support from the press. Nobody knew about them, let alone willing to help them.

The difference was that Orville and Wilbur were driven by something deeper than money. They were driven by a cause, a purpose, a belief that if they were to create the first flying machine, it would change the course of the world.

Samuel Pierpont Langley was different. He was driven by a desire to be rich and famous. He was in pursuit of the result and the riches and didn't really care about the cause. This was none more so demonstrated than when he found out the Wright brothers had taken flight—he quit the very same day! He could have applauded their achievement, tried to improve upon it to make it even better, but he wasn't interested. He didn't get rich or famous and so he quit.

People are driven not simply by what you do, but why you do it. Communicating this is key to driving high performance in those around you.

People are drawn into an emotional cause. If you communicate in an emotional way, you will attract the people to help you with your cause and you will also get commitment and a will to go the extra mile for you, where all the money and rationality just won't do the same job.

Somebody who captured the power of this superbly was Martin Luther King.

In 1963, Martin Luther King gave a speech which has since reverberated around the world many times over. You probably know the speech I am talking about, and 250,000 people showed up to hear it. A quarter of a million people!

Interestingly, he wasn't the only person in America who had suffered due to the lack of civil rights, he wasn't the only great communicator of his day, and he certainly didn't have all the answers on how to tackle the problem.

On top of that, there were no invitations sent out, no emails or social media to remind people. Why, then, did so many people show up to hear what he had to say? What was so different about King?

King spoke from the heart. He didn't go around telling people what needed to change or how to fix problems; he told people what he believed.

"I believe, I believe, I believe…"

He shared his core beliefs, his deepest desires; he shared his "dream". He didn't share his detailed strategy and ten-point plan, he shared his dream. He communicated from his heart and connected with people at an emotional level. Those who shared the same beliefs as King all turned up to hear what he had to say. They followed him and his cause.

People are driven by emotion much more so than by logic. If you want people to buy into your message, make sure it connects at a deeper level.

When people are engaged at a deeper emotional level, they will perform at a higher level and they will give more for the cause.

An example of this is a large pharmaceutical company I did some work for, working with one of their sales teams under a lot of pressure to deliver. We shifted their focus from the nuts and bolts of the day job—"selling drugs to doctors"—to the difference they made—"saving patients' lives."

The result?

They over-delivered on expectations, beating targets by over 160 percent.

Purpose driven.

Somebody else who understood the power of this was Clive Woodward, who guided the England Rugby team to World Cup glory in 2003. Prior to this, England Rugby had suffered. They had performed badly and had been vilified in the press, and public interest certainly wasn't widespread across the nation. Woodward, assisted by Humphrey Walters set out with a new cause to get people interested:

"Our duty was to inspire the nation so that all the people who maybe don't like rugby, they'll tell us they remember where they were and who they were with when we won the World Cup. So I said that means that all our behaviours, work ethic, everything, has got to say 'I'm participating in inspiring the nation.'"

With this cause, they did just that, achieving the dream and capturing the nation at the same time. Here is Humphrey again on what it takes to make a great leader:

"All the great leaders…most of them, have started with a desire to do something for other people. I think you've got to have that. It's not money. The second thing they have is an amazing ability to get people to like them and follow them, by being true to their word. I think the third, and probably the most important thing, is they know what the process is and then they find people to help them and practise. They're not frightened to go out and ask other people."

Somebody else in sport who knows about the power of a common purpose is Sir Alex Ferguson. Ferguson used the power of stories to communicate with his players, to get them bought in on an emotional level:

"I like to tell different stories, and use my imagination. But generally, it is about our expectations, their belief in themselves, and their trust in each other."

One such story is the one of three stone masons.

One day, a man is walking by a building site and comes across several stone masons working away. Intrigued about what they are working on, he asks three of them.

The first mason looks rather distracted and fed up. "Chipping away at this big block of stone," he says.

The second mason, looking a little more enthused, replies, "I am cutting this stone down to shape to build this wall."

The third mason, working away diligently with great focus, stops what he's doing, and with his eyes lighting up, he tells the man, "We here are building a great cathedral."

Ferguson always talked about Manchester United Football Club: the history, the great managers of the past, and keeping up with the great traditions of the club.

No one player was ever as big as Manchester United the club.

His communication to his players was one and the same to keep them engaged and focused on being part of the great history, of creating history for themselves, and not just collecting a nice salary.

What time is it?

If we go back to the research done by Jim Collins and his colleagues on what makes great companies, he said that the great companies were "clock builders and not time tellers".

The difference is, if you build a clock, you won't need to keep telling people the time. You will leave something to do that for you.

All the great leaders I have studied so far for this book have this in common. It is about making a difference and leaving something for people that will outlast themselves, something that lasts long after they have played their part.

What are you leaving behind?

What will your legacy be?

What difference are you trying to make?

Make sure you are engaging people on an emotional level with your message and, first and foremost, that you are engaged with the *why* of what you're doing yourself.

Write a story worth telling one day.

Think about the *why* behind what you do and make some notes below.

Are you engaged only at a surface level or is there a deeper purpose and meaning to your work?

The more you reflect on this, the clearer your answers will be.

Intrinsically Tuned

"In any given moment we have two options: to step forward into growth or to step back into safety."

Abraham Maslow

Now we have a basic understanding of the workings of the human brain and what drives our behaviour, let's take a deeper look at what science teaches us about motivation.

We have to go all the way back to the 1930's, to Henry Vilas Zoological park, where two psychologists, Abraham Maslow and Harry Harlow, began studying monkeys.

The use of monkeys as research tools in brain science and psychology grew out of the similarity in the brain development of humans and primates.

At this point, some psychologists believed there were only two main drives for human behaviour—the biological drive to survive, and the need to seek rewards and avoid punishment.

While Maslow moved on from studying the monkeys, Harlow stayed.

Maslow, unlike other psychologists at the time, was interested in studying the positive qualities of people rather than the bad qualities, and was often critical of people like Sigmund Freud for doing so.

In 1943, Maslow proposed his theory on human motivation, stating that people had five human needs they needed to fulfil for psychological health.

The basic needs for survival, followed by the higher needs for fulfilment, built on the basic drives that had already been explored.

While Maslow was working on his motivation theory, Harlow was still experimenting with monkeys and, interestingly, finding similarly that people have a higher need for satisfaction.

In 1949, he conducted an experiment with eight monkeys, placing them in a cage with a puzzle to see how they reacted. According to what they knew at the time about motivation, the monkeys would have no desire to solve the puzzles unless there was a reason to do so.

So they were surprised when, almost immediately, the monkeys began playing with the puzzles and had not long after figured out how to complete them.

Their survival didn't depend on it and they were not being punished or rewarded in any way.

Harlow offered the following theory on why they completed the puzzle:

"The performance of the task provided intrinsic reward."

The monkeys performed because they found it gratifying to solve puzzles. They enjoyed it, and the joy of the task was its own reward.

This led Harlow to propose that there was a third drive in human motivation, which is an intrinsic drive—to achieve an internal feeling of satisfaction.

Further experiments found that offering external rewards to solve these puzzles didn't improve performance and often disrupted the completion of the task.

Twenty years later, with no more work done on this theory, a young psychologist by the name of Edward Deci followed up on Harlow's studies on intrinsic motivation and ran a series of experiments to see what happened to people's performance when rewards were introduced.

What they found surprised many behavioural scientists at the time and backed up what Harlow had found 20 years earlier.

In one experiment, where they offered students cash prizes to solves puzzles, he found that once they had been offered a financial reward for completing the puzzles, their future motivation for them faded. The results suggested that although financial rewards can offer short term motivation, the effect wears off, and, even worse, the rewards can reduce a person's longer-term interest and motivation for the task.

Deci proposed that human beings have an inherent tendency to seek out challenge, to explore, and to learn. This drive, however, is more fragile than other drives, and we have to carefully manage and tune into it if we are to get people intrinsically motivated and engaged at a higher level.

Years later, in 1985, Edward Deci and another psychologist, Richard Ryan, developed what has proven to be one of the most influential and widely accepted theories of human motivation. They called it Self-Determination Theory (SDT).

The theory states that human beings have three innate psychological needs that need fulfilling for optimal performance and motivation.

These needs are for the following:

Competence: The need to feel effective at meeting everyday challenges and opportunities. Learning and using skills.

Relatedness: The need to interact, to connect with others, and to experience caring.

Autonomy: A sense of control over our own lives; the need to feel that we have choices.

Beyond the basic needs proposed in Maslow's hierarchy of needs, the similarities between the two theories are quite apparent.

There has been lots of fascinating research carried out in many different environments to test the effectiveness of SDT. If we understand this research in its basic terms, then we can use it to engage people at a higher level, ultimately maximising their performance by understanding what innately makes them tick.

In the zone.

You hear this phrase used a lot, especially in sport. Growing up playing sport, I heard this phrase bandied about an awful lot long before I knew where it came from, but I still had a sense of what it meant.

The definition I like is "complete absorption in what one does".

The term comes from a psychologist called Mihaly Csikszentmihalyi who, in the 1970's, became fascinated by artists who would essentially get lost in their work. Some of them were so immersed in what they were doing that they would often disregard their need for food, water and even sleep (basic needs).

The term he came up with for these people who found themselves "lost in the moment" was "flow". He carried out numerous studies on various people experiencing a state of flow and reported it to be the highest, most satisfying state people could experience. A state where time almost feels like it has stopped, completely absorbed in the moment with intense focus and satisfaction.

Flow has been widely researched and recognised throughout history and many cultures. Sport talks of being "in the zone", meditation talks of "being in the present moment", and Buddhism talks of "the art of non-doing", all closely resembling the state of flow.

Psychologists state that there is limited amount of information our mind can attend to at any one time. Mihaly states that it is about 110 bits of information per second, which may seem like an awful lot of information, and once again demonstrates the power of the human brain.

Beyond our basic drives, most people are able to consciously decide where to place their attention. Mihaly states that when somebody is in flow, they are so immersed in the task at hand that they lose awareness of all other things, including time, people, distractions, and even basic bodily needs.

As you can imagine, flow is a powerful and productive state of mind to be in. I have experienced it several times when writing this book, where I just completely forget my surroundings and the fact that I haven't had a drink for several hours.

The question then becomes: how do you get there more often?

A flow state can be entered while performing a variety of activities, although the chances of it happening are much higher when you are performing the task for intrinsic purposes, in line with the research noted above. There are three conditions that have to be met in order to achieve a flow state according to the theory:

1. You must be involved in an activity with a clear set of goals and progress, giving direction and structure to the task.
2. The task must have clear and immediate feedback.
3. You must have a good balance between the perceived challenge of the task and your own perceived level of skill. You must have confidence in your ability to complete the task.

In 1987, Mihaly and his team created the following chart (the Experience Fluctuation Model) to depict eight states that are possible when negotiating the balance between challenge and skill. Getting this balance right is the key to getting into a flow state:

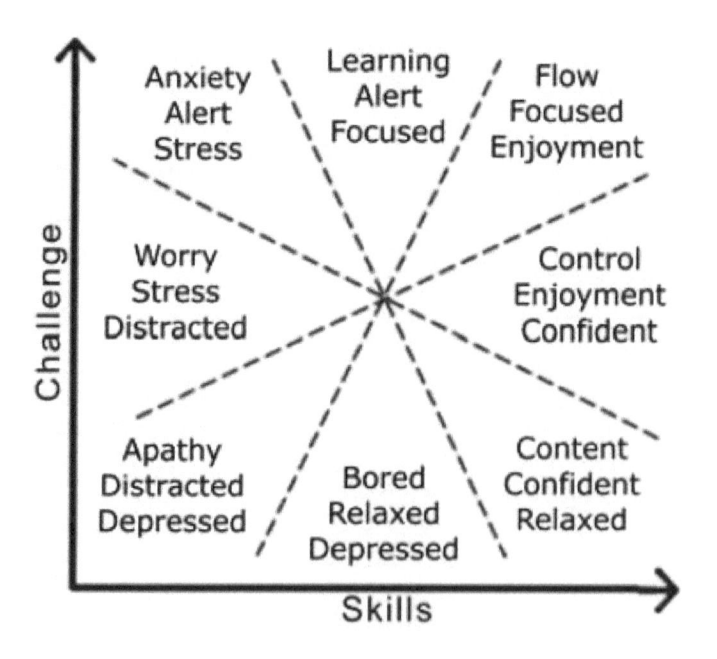

```
                  Learning
        Anxiety    Alert      Flow
         Alert    Focused    Focused
        Stress              Enjoyment

   Challenge
         Worry                Control
        Stress              Enjoyment
       Distracted            Confident


        Apathy                Content
       Distracted   Bored    Confident
       Depressed  Relaxed     Relaxed
                 Depressed
                   Skills →
```

As you can see, if somebody with a low level of skill in a particular task is set a challenge too high, they will feel stressed and likely under-perform.

Alternatively, if somebody who has a high skill level is set a challenge too low, they will likely get bored and distracted quickly, again leading to low performance.

The key is matching the level of challenge to the level of skill. Those with a higher skill level are more likely to enter into a state of flow.

The joy of the journey.

Remember earlier when I introduced you to the work of the psychologist Carol Dweck and her research around the importance of a "growth mindset"?

Can you see the similarities here?

People who have a growth mindset thrive on challenge and developing themselves. They are intrinsically motivated by the challenge of the task, by growing and developing, and are not just focused on the end result.

There are some clear themes and patterns emerging from all of this research, which gives it even more credibility, as it has been tested and proven over many decades by different researchers in different industries on all types of people (and animals).

But how can you use this knowledge to your advantage?

Dweck states the case for learning goals over performance goals. The difference being, learning goals are focused on increasing your competence (remember Deci's theory). Learning goals are aligned with the desire to learn new skills and gain mastery and self-esteem.

Performance goals, on the other hand, are focused entirely on the result, meaning they are about winning positive judgements and avoiding negative ones, according to Dweck. Being overly concerned with looking good and avoiding ridicule leads to people playing it safe and not performing as well as they are capable.

In one particular study in 1988, Dweck and her team measured the impact of performance goals and learning goals on student performance in a series of tests.

The students who were given performance goals showed a clear helpless response when they faced difficulty. They criticised their own ability and their performance got worse.

On the flip side, those who were set learning goals showed that even in the face of failure, their heads did not fall. They remained focused on the task, worked longer, and scored higher.

They found that when the students were more focused on learning, failure was likely to provoke continued effort instead of dejection and discouragement.

How do you set goals?

Are you more focused on learning or the end results?

How can you structure your goals to optimise the growth mindset?

Pablo Picasso, the famous artist, was somebody who clearly understood the importance of having an inside-out approach to his work, knowing that a focus on mastery eventually leads to great results.

In one of my favourite stories that I have heard about him, a lady walking down the street in France in the early 1900's noticed Picasso painting in the street. She approached him gently, first confirming it was him, then asking him if he would mind sketching her a quick portrait. He duly obliged and, thirty seconds later, handed her a piece of paper. He said, "Now be careful with that, because one day it will be worth a fortune."

She said, "But it's only taken you thirty seconds."

To which he responded, "Yes, but it has taken me thirty years to produce that in thirty seconds."

"Make each day your masterpiece."

The words above are a fitting end to this chapter from one of the most revered coaches in the history of sport, John Wooden.

Wooden led UCLA to ten championships in twelve years, including seven in a row. No other team has ever won more than two in a row. His achievements were extraordinary. In his first year, his team were predicted to finish bottom of the division and they ended up as champions.

What principles did Wooden apply to inspire such extraordinary feats from his players, year after year?

Firstly, he stated that as long as his players gave their best effort, then they could never lose, regardless of the score. He was relentlessly focused on daily increments in performance, knowing that the small gains each day all add up.

And, perhaps most tellingly of all, Wooden was most passionate about developing his players and helping them to fulfil their potential—not just in basketball, but in life in general.

Can you get a sense of what it would have been like to play for him?

I know I can, and of course it's no surprise that his players gave him everything in return.

Stop Monkeying Around

"Action is the foundational key to all success"
Pablo Picasso

In 1952, on the island of Koshima near the far south of Japan, a tribe of monkeys were to play their part in a social phenomenon. The monkeys were used to eating fruit from trees until a group of scientists buried sweet potatoes in the sand and waited to see how they reacted.

The monkeys enjoyed the taste of the sweet potato, but the sand and dirt would prevent them from eating them. At least initially it did.

One day, a young female monkey found a way to solve the problem by washing the potatoes in a nearby stream. The young monkey then taught her mother to do the same so she too could enjoy the potatoes. Soon enough, her friends and their families learned too, until more and more monkeys were following the same behaviour.

Then, one day, it happened. The scientists observed that when the number of monkeys following the behaviour reached 100, all of the monkeys on the island followed suit. And it didn't stop there, with the behaviour eventually spreading to other islands.

The scientists observed that once the number of monkeys reached a critical number, in this case 100, the behaviour then caught on with momentum.

Although the exact number may vary, the "hundredth monkey effect", as it was called, demonstrates that there is a critical point for a new idea or way of doing things to catch on, meaning that once your lead catches on, it will soon enough become the commonly accepted way.

But only if someone goes first.

As easy as ABC.

The research so far highlights the importance of our emotional state on the way we behave. Taking charge of the way we behave is key to driving the results we want to create. Therefore, taking charge of our emotional state is key not only to being an inspirational leader, but also to making sure we have a rich and positive experience of life.

I have identified three key things that have a direct influence on our emotional state. Taking charge of each of these areas will help you to consistently influence the way you feel. I call it the ABC Formula.

The ABC Formula.

I have created the ABC Formula to help you take the ideas presented in this book and put them into practice.

Attention: Where do you focus your attention?

Behaviour: What action will you now take?

Commentary: What are you saying to yourself, and what impact does this have?

ATTENTION

The book started off talking about the power of our perceptions, and how these drive our experiences and our behaviours. We learned that our mind is a complex mechanism and we often miss the most obvious and simple things.

We learned about the power of our expectations, not just on ourselves, but also the impact they have on other people's behaviour. Remember the study on children's performance in school, the Pygmalion effect?

What we pay attention to has a powerful effect.

Are you paying attention to the right things?

We learned about the power of our different brains and the battle between them. The rational, thinking brain is the one I want to focus on in this section, because this is the conscious part of our brain, meaning that it allows us take control of what we focus on.

When we take control of what we focus on, we can radically influence our own performance and the performance of those around us.

But let's take a look at why this isn't easy for most people.

Our first and most important primary function in life is to survive. This primal drive means that our brain is always (below our awareness) on the lookout for potential threats and dangers to our survival. You can imagine how powerful this software is.

Consequently, our brain is wired to notice and record the negative events in our lives more powerfully than the positive events.

Let me share this common example with you to explain what I mean:

Imagine you go to work on a typical day and throughout the course of the day, ten things go really well, but one thing goes horribly wrong.

What do you drive home thinking about?

What do you spend the next day thinking about?

How much of the good stuff can you now recall?

The point is, it doesn't come naturally to vibrantly recall the good events like the negative ones. Our brains are not wired to dwell on the positives.

Now, what does this have to do with inspiring great performance?

'Learn from your mistakes'

Learning from your mistakes is absolutely essential to success. So we are told.

But according to Clive Woodward, the man who lead the England Rugby team to World Cup glory in 2003 against all the odds, we must be smart about this.

"I prefer to concentrate on success."

When he took over the England Rugby team, he found a culture like many in the business and sports worlds. One where when you win, you celebrate. And when you lose, you ponder.

He says the smart boss is the one who knows that if you win, that is when you get called in for the early meeting. Not the other way around.

He switched this culture, meaning they were now to place more focus on what went well, because success breeds success.

"When you've won it's easy to say 'Great, let's have a couple of days off.' But that's when you must redouble your efforts. That's what I've done with this team. We've never overreacted to a loss. I prefer to concentrate on success."

So when you lose? "Go on the piss!" he laughs.

In other words, learn from it quickly and move on. Shift your focus.

It is too easy to get caught up dwelling on all the things that go wrong. And of course, things will go wrong all the time.

What you pay attention to is your choice.

What you pay attention to drives how you feel.

How you feel influences the decisions you make and the actions you take.

Eliminate the negatives?

In 2000, two economics professors, Uri Gneezy and Aldo Rustichini, studied a childcare facility in Israel over a twenty-week period. The centre opened at 7.30 a.m. and closed at 4.00 p.m. Each day, the children's parents had to collect their children by 4.00 p.m., otherwise the teachers would have to stay late.

During the first four weeks, the economist recorded how often the parents were late. Then at the start of the fifth week, they introduced a fine for parents who were late.

The theory behind this is that if you want a behaviour to be reduced, then punish the negative behaviour.

What actually happened after they introduced the fine was that more parents started coming late for their children! After a few weeks, the number of parents who were now coming late had doubled. This obviously shocked the researchers, as they had not even considered this as an outcome.

One of the main reasons why the parents showed up on time was the relationship they had with the teacher. It was in their interest to be on good terms with them, given the influence they had on their children. When the fine was introduced, this switched the focus from an internal drive to a now external drive. Rather than the internal drive of being moral and maintaining a relationship (emotional), now they were doing it to avoid a fine, essentially making it more transactional and less meaningful (rational).

Putting the emphasis here on the negative only created more of it, instead of looking to focus on and reward parents for showing up on time and encouraging this behaviour.

What can we learn from this?

Promote and encourage the behaviour you want to see more of. What you focus on is more likely to occur.

Edward Deci, who founded Self-Determination Theory, found that giving people unexpected positive feedback on a task increases their intrinsic motivation to do it, because the positive feedback fulfils their need for competence.

On the flip side, research also shows that negative feedback has the opposite effect, decreasing people's intrinsic motivation for what they do.

But can praise be harmful?

If we look once more at the research done by Carol Dweck and her team on encouraging a growth mindset, one which every high-performance culture could benefit from, then we must be careful about what element of the performance we praise.

Dweck ran a series of tests with children, praising some of the children for their results. For example, they praised them for the score they got and then told them that they must be very smart or talented ("Wow. You got eight out of ten correct. That's a great score. You must be really smart.").

They praised others for their effort ("Wow. You got eight correct. That's a great score. You must have worked really hard for this.").

Both groups performed equally to begin with, but right after the praise, they started to differ. The group who were praised for their ability were pushed into the fixed mindset and displayed all the telling signs.

When they were now offered another opportunity to learn from a challenging new task, they rejected it, as they were fearful of exposing any flaws or having their talent questioned.

In contrast, the students who were praised for their effort accepted the new challenging task 90 percent of the time, meaning they ended up learning more and continually improving.

Dweck made an important observation following her research. People thought they could just hand out praise for effort and see the same effects. Not so easy. The praise only worked when the children actually tried; it cannot be faked.

So, before you go off being that person who everybody sees through when they throw praise at everything, just make sure it is coming from a place of integrity and not a place of manipulation.

People have a great radar for BS!

This means: pay attention to people's effort. Help them to grow. Put the Pygmalion effect to use (like Steve Jobs did) by seeing their potential and pushing them to work hard.

And, of course, be the example.

Be careful with rewards.

In the 1970's, a wooden puzzle called Soma gained huge popularity, and Edward Deci and his colleagues used it to test the effect of rewards on people's motivation.

Deci divided students into two groups and placed each group in a room with a Soma puzzle and some magazines. He asked the students to play with the puzzle for thirty minutes. Before he started the experiment, he told one group that if they could solve the puzzle in the allotted time then they would get a financial reward, whilst the other group were offered no incentive to complete the puzzle.

After the time was up, he told them he needed to attend to something and would be back in about ten minutes with a questionnaire. This is when the experiment really begun. Deci then observed what the students did in this time.

There was a significant difference in the behaviours of each group. The group who had been offered the financial reward for participating in the puzzle picked up the magazines to read, while the group who had been offered no reward were much more likely to continue playing with the puzzle.

The findings of this study sparked other researchers to carry out similar experiments. In one of the most well-known studies of this nature, Stanford psychologist Mark Lepper and his team visited several schools armed with crayons and paper and gave children the task of drawing some pictures.

One group were told they would receive a reward for participating, a "good player" certificate, while another group were not told of any reward at all.

A few weeks later, Lepper and his team returned to the school armed with crayons again and measured how many children played with them. The groups who had received the certificates the last time around spent significantly less time drawing than those who never received a reward.

The British psychologist Richard Wiseman tells a story of a wise old man who captured the essence of this knowledge and used it cunningly to his advantage.

The wise old man lived in an area with troublesome youths who had a habit of causing trouble. One day, they turned up outside his home and started shouting abuse at him for no reason. In the days following, they would turn up outside his house and shout abuse over and over again. Now, many old men would have decided the best course of action would be to call the police. The wise old man knew better.

He thought of a much smarter way to combat the problem.

The following day when the abusive youths turn up, he was sat outside his home waiting for them. He told them that he enjoyed them shouting abuse at him and he was even willing to pay them for it!

Stunned, the youths took the wise man's money and shouted the usual abuse. Each day, the wise man would repeat the same process, offering them money to shout their abuse.

The following week, the wise old man told the youths that he didn't have much money this time and could only pay them a tiny amount.

Slightly surprised and angered with this, they continued with their abuse, but maybe lacking the usual edge.

At the start of the following week, it all changed. This time, the wise old man told them he was so broke, he could only pay them pennies for their abuse. Now, the youths really weren't happy. A few pence? For all this trouble we go to? No chance! And they disappeared, never to return again.

What can we learn from this?

In the studies done in this area, when rewards were offered to complete a task, the focus switched from the joy of the task itself and turned it into a chore rather than a joy. You could say the motivation became "have to", not "want to", and of course when we feel we have to do something, it becomes less interesting and desirable.

Rewards are offered in the hope that the person's motivation and desire for the task will increase, not realising that they are more likely to drain that person's intrinsic motivation. Rewards often work in the short-term, but if you want lasting motivation, focus more on making the task enjoyable.

To get the best out of people and sustain high performance, you will get better results if you create an environment that people can flourish in.

Give them adequate challenges that match their skill level.

Help them to grow as people with training and development.

Help them to see the difference they make—the WHY.

Give meaningful and carefully selected praise focused on effort, not talent.

Can you see how the suggestions above are rewards too? Just not in the traditional sense. Then again, high performance cultures aren't all that traditional.

BEHAVIOUR

William James was the first person to teach a psychology course in America. Often referred to as the father of American psychology, James was considered the country's greatest philosopher. His contribution to the field of psychology still lives on today, and his controversial theories back then have gathered much pace since.

James is probably most known for his theory on emotion (the James-Lange theory). In his book *The Principles of Psychology*, James said, "Common sense says we lose our fortune, are sorry and weep; we meet a bear, are frightened and run; we are insulted by a rival, are angry and strike. The hypothesis here to be defended says that the order of sequence is incorrect…that we feel sorry because we cry, angry because we strike, afraid because we tremble…"

What James was saying was that our presumption is that we experience our emotions based on what we experience and how we think about it. The James-Lange theory proposes the opposite, hence the resistance and criticism his theory faced.

But was his theory totally absurd?

Do we smile because we feel happy?

Or do we feel happy because we smile?

James wasn't your traditional psychologist. He found experiments boring and unrewarding, and so he never formally tested his theory. Therefore, it lacked the research to prove its credibility.

Fast forward to the 1960's, to the work of a young psychologist, James Laird, studying at the University of Rochester. One day, Laird observed one of his clients smiling in a peculiar way and wondered where the smile came from and how he was feeling at the time.

"For some reason, I tried smiling the way that guy did. It didn't help. So I asked myself, 'How do I smile?' I smiled in my way and then I thought, 'I feel happy.' Then I tried scowling and gritting my teeth and that made me feel angry. Then I frowned and that made me feel depressed. So I thought, 'That's funny. It's not supposed to happen that way.' We all know the feeling is supposed to cause the behaviour, not the other way around. But that's not what I was experiencing."

After this event, Laird read up on as much about emotion as he could, and came across William James and his theory. Whereas James had no real interest, Laird decided to find out if James' theory was right by putting it to the test.

He started with an experiment where he got people to smile, followed by asking them how they felt. "The experiment had to involve a great deal of disguise. If I asked you to smile and then asked you how you feel, you'd know what I want you to say. So I needed a decoy."

The decoy he used was electrodes. Laird put electrodes on people's faces at the corners of the mouth, corners of the jaw, and between the eyebrows. He disguised his real research aims by telling the participants that he was measuring the electrical activity in the electrodes, when in fact, they were never turned on. He asked them to relax and contract their facial muscles into a smile or a frown, once again disguised by getting them to create the facial expression without telling them to actually smile or frown. Once they had done so, they would complete a questionnaire, selecting a list of emotions they felt at the time.

The results reflected his experience that day driving home in the car. He found that people felt significantly happier when they forced their face into a smile, and significantly angrier when they forced their face into a frown.

Laird carried out dozens of similar experiments, testing the theory of whether the way we feel drives how we behave, or the other way around.

In one fascinating study, he wanted to test the effects of self-esteem on decision making. Traditional research shows us that people with low self-esteem are more likely to make demeaning choices in their lives.

In the study, he got the subjects to first complete a questionnaire about self-esteem. Then he took them to a room where they would sit down at a table. On the table were some cooking weights, a knife and fork, and a live worm.

The subjects were then asked to take part in one of two exercises, decided by the toss of a coin. One of them was placing the weights in escalating order, and the other was chopping the worm up and eating it.

When the coin was tossed, subjects were told which task to prepare for. The subjects would then prepare (and brace!) themselves to either sort the weights or eat the worm, and just before they were about to do so, they were asked to quickly fill out another questionnaire.

Laird predicted that those people who saw themselves about to carry out a demeaning experience (eating a worm) would be more likely to believe they had low self-esteem, and the questionnaire would confirm this. He was right: the self-esteem results of the worm eaters dropped significantly in the second questionnaire.

Then, after completing the questionnaire and about to tuck into the demeaning experience of eating the worm, the experimenter gasps and shouts "Stop!", conceding that they have made a terrible mistake. You should have in fact been given a choice about which task to choose—the weights or eating the worm.

Laird knew that people with self-esteem often believe they deserve bad experiences, and he was interested to discover whether the experiment-induced low self-esteem would alter the subjects' behaviour.

He found that none of the subjects who had been assigned to the weights switched to eating the worm. No surprises there, then!

But, even though the worm eaters had the choice of switching to a much more pleasurable task, 80 percent of them chose to eat the worm!

In the same way that smiling led to people feeling happier, taking part in a demeaning experience led people to develop lower self-esteem and make a more demeaning choice in the future.

What can we learn from this?

Well, in the words of William James, "If you want a quality, act as if you already had it."

In other words, if you want to feel confident, act confident.

If you want to feel happier, smile more.

If you want to feel better about yourself, act in the way you would if you felt great.

Often, we can get too caught up in the way we feel before we are willing to act, whereas the most effective thing we can do is act, and then the feeling arrives afterwards.

I have often experienced that writing this book. Not necessarily feeling very creative or inspired to write, I have forced myself to sit down and just begin small, and, after a short while, the creative juices have started to flow and I'm fully in the zone.

Four minutes to prove yourself.

Research shows that it takes four minutes to make a first impression, and, according to a widely-cited study by UCLA professor Albert Mehrabian, body language accounts for 55 percent of that impression (38 percent comes from tone of voice, and the remaining 7 percent from our actual words).

There were flaws in this research so it cannot always be applied to every situation, but it certainly can serve as a benchmark for understanding the elements of our communication.

What is the importance of a positive first impression?

A Harvard study showed it takes eight subsequent positive encounters to change somebody's negative impression of you. Make it easier for yourself by getting off to a good start.

And if body language accounts for so much of our communication, then it matters much more not what we say, but how we say it. Not just our words, but the expression on our face.

How do you greet people when you meet them?

Do you give people your full attention?

Do you smile at people? Look them in the eye?

Do you stand tall and exude the confidence of a leader with your body language, even when you sometimes don't feel it?

All of these small steps make a difference; the research is there to prove it.

I feel good, I knew that I would…

Ultimately, people want to feel good, and when they do, they perform better. But sometimes, no matter how good we want to feel, those feelings can be hard to come by.

Therefore, heed the advice of the great William James and try acting your way into feeling good.

You may not "feel" like giving somebody the praise they deserve. Act as if you are.

You may not "feel" like challenging people to fulfil their potential. Act as if you are.

You may not "feel" confident about your upcoming presentation. Act as if you are.

The feelings will soon follow.

Some people may feel that this is inauthentic. How can you act in a certain way if you don't feel like it? In situations such as this, use your moral compass to guide you. Is it the right thing to do? Will behaving in a positive manner help the situation? If the answer is yes, then act your way through. The best leaders have to do things they don't always feel like doing for the good of those around them.

Have a think about the behaviours you display when you are performing at your best. If you find it hard to think of them, ask somebody you trust and who knows you well.

Now complete the exercise on the next page.

List your top five behaviours:

1.

2.

3.

4.

5.

You can also do this for your team. What five behaviours would I see from you if you were performing at your very best?

Now, in order to remind yourself of how you act when you are at your very best, list these behaviours where you and/or your team will see them every day, until they become automatic.

COMMENTARY

Earlier, I discussed the work of Martin Seligman, a pioneer in the field of positive psychology who coined the term "learned helplessness" to describe someone's reaction in a situation where they felt powerless to change.

Later, Seligman stated that each person has their own explanatory style which has a large influence on how much they are affected by learned helplessness.

Your explanatory style determines how you explain events to yourself, both positive and negative. According to Seligman, people who generally tend to blame themselves for negative events, believe that these events will continue to happen, and let them affect many other aspects of their lives, display what is called a pessimistic explanatory style. People who display the pessimistic style tend to respond to events from a position of personal helplessness.

Conversely, people who generally tend to blame outside forces for negative events, believe that such events will end soon, and do not let these events affect too many aspects of their lives, display what is called an optimistic explanatory style. People who display the optimistic style tend to respond to events from a position of personal power.

It is important to note that people can display elements of both styles, depending on the situation.

In the mid 1980's, Seligman started looking at the performance of professional sports teams in America and predicting their success with great accuracy. He was reading and listening to interviews in which the coaches and players would talk about their performance and listening for their language to determine whether it hinted at an optimistic or a pessimistic style.

He found that the teams who displayed an optimistic style showed a greater response to failure and, therefore, achieved more success than predicted in following seasons.

In 1988, he got an opportunity to work with the US swim team ahead of the Olympic Games in South Korea. Seligman had all of the swimmers complete a questionnaire which would question them about their response to challenges. This questionnaire, without them knowing, would then predict their explanatory style on a range from pessimistic to optimistic.

One swimmer in the team, Matt Biondi, scored as highly optimistic. The coach later asked the swimmers to swim a timed lap, but instead of giving them their actual time, the swimmers were given a fake time. One that was slow enough to disappoint them, but not so bad that they would dispute it.

Seligman wanted to monitor their response to disappointment. In the following training session, when the swimmers were given their times, they were told to swim the lap again. The second time around, those who scored as having a pessimistic style recorded even worse times. Meanwhile, those who were rated as optimistic improved their times, with Biondi, who scored as the most optimistic, recording the fastest time.

Overall, optimists either maintained or improved performance after disappointment. Pessimists deteriorated by two seconds in a 100-yard event, which is the difference between first and last place in their event.

When the team went to the Olympics, Biondi was a large favourite and was predicted to win seven gold medals. In his first race, he finished in third place. He improved upon this in his second race, but only to take silver. You can imagine what people were now saying about him being able to cope with the expectation. Biondi was not deterred by his underperformance and remained optimistic for the final five races, bringing home gold in every one and setting four world records in the process.

Optimism in the workplace.

In 1985, Seligman started working with Metropolitan Life Insurance Company. He found that insurance agents were a highly optimistic group. Fifteen thousand people took a questionnaire to determine their style, and performance was later measured to see the impact of optimism on their success.

The more optimistic half of agents studied sold 37% more than the pessimistic half.

The most optimistic 10% sold **88%** more than the most pessimistic 10%.

The pessimistic half was two times as likely to quit in the first year.

The most pessimistic quarter was three times as likely to quit in the first year.

Optimism defined.

The case for having an optimistic attitude is really strong. But what does it mean to be optimistic?

There are three key elements which your style is measured on:

Permanence

Optimists believe bad events are temporary setbacks, and this is reflected in what they tell themselves when things don't go to plan, i.e. "Things haven't been going my way lately" or "It didn't go to plan this time".

Pessimists believe that bad events hold permanence, and this is also reflected in what they tell themselves following events that don't go well, i.e. "Things never go my way." or "Plans never work out."

Conversely, when things do go well, the order is reversed. Optimists tend to describe these events as permanent ("I always perform when it matters.") versus the temporary explanation used by those with the pessimistic style ("I don't know how I pulled that off.").

To increase your chances of success, make sure you and your team are using temporary language to explain events that go wrong, and permanent language when events go well.

Can you see the link here to the words of Clive Woodward when he said he was more interested in focusing on success, and not what went wrong, when the England Rugby team lost?

Pervasiveness

This refers to one's tendency to generalise when things go wrong. Those with the pessimistic style tend to generalise more ("They always do that." and "I'm stupid."), increasing the chance of poor performance having a knock-on negative effect in other areas.

Those with an optimistic style tend to use more specific language, isolating the situation and preventing it from affecting other areas ("They said no." and "I failed an exam.").

You can begin to imagine the effect on overall performance when people reduce the generalisations they use when events don't go well.

Personalisation

This refers to one's tendency to make it personal and blame themselves when things don't go well. Pessimists tend to blame themselves, to make it personal and all about them, which is damaging to their self-esteem ("It's all my fault." or "I totally messed that up.").

Optimists, on the other hand, tend to externalise negative events by finding conditions which help to explain why things went wrong ("The market conditions didn't help." or "There wasn't enough time to perfect it.").

It is important to distinguish here that taking ownership for our mistakes is important, but there is a clear difference between that and blaming ourselves, which is much more severe and destructive.

In a team environment, listen out for the language when things go wrong, and who and what people blame. People blaming other people can lead to obvious problems, but finding reasons outside of each other will mean you bounce back quicker without a damaging effect on people's morale.

Prisoner of war.

Being an optimist is not just about hope like some people are led to believe. Optimism is grounded in much greater mental strength than that. It is not about blindly hoping and believing something will happen, it is about making a decision that you will find a way to make it happen even when things start turning against you.

In the book *Good to Great*, Jim Collins uses the story of Jim Stockdale to exemplify this point. Jim Stockdale was a US Navy vice admiral who was awarded a medal of honour in the Vietnam War, where he was held prisoner for seven and a half years. He was part of the so-called "Alcatraz Gang", US prisoners who were held in solitary confinement for all of that time. The lights in their cells were kept on twenty-four hours a day and they were forced to sleep in shackles.

When Collins interviewed him about his time in the camps and his coping strategy for survival, Stockdale told him that he never doubted that he would get out and he would turn the experience into the defining event of his life. He found a way to give the event meaning and use it in a positive sense, even in the most drastic of circumstances.

Stockdale said the prisoners who never survived were blindly optimistic. Hoping they would be out at Christmas, and then deflated when it didn't happen. Then hanging onto the hope it would be Easter, and that never happened. By the time it got back around to Christmas again, these prisoners had died of a broken heart.

He said in order to survive, you needed to always have faith that you would prevail in the end, but mix it with the discipline to confront the most brutal facts of your current reality, whatever they might be.

Stockdale did that, and he received a medal of honour for his courage. Real optimism breeds resilience, and is about having the courage to face the brutal facts whilst keeping faith in reaching the finish line.

Use the ABC Formula.

Put these principles into practice every day, using the ABC Formula to drive high performance and keep yourself in an empowering, emotional state of mind.

Make sure you are more focused on the things that are going well.

Focus on the end game; never let your faith in the result waiver.

Find more reasons for prevailing than you do for failing.

This will take some practise because the brain is wired to notice the negatives first, remember. Start meetings with the positives, start the day with the positives, start your conversations with the positives. It is too easy to be sucked into the negatives and have them take over, which will drain the spirit from you and those around you.

Also, pay attention to where people's attention is going. Just be aware of this and make subtle changes. Be careful not to pick people up on this too heavily; most won't even know they are doing it because it comes so naturally. Just listen and steer people in the right direction. Highlighting the negatives too much will only increase the frequency of them happening!

Make a conscious effort to display your best behaviours each day, even in the situations when you don't feel like it. When you do this, your emotional state will begin to change. The brain is a complex organ and we don't always feel inspired and motivated to do our best. In these situations, don't ruminate on this, just act. Positive action breeds positive results, which in turn breeds positive feelings.

And finally, be more aware of your own self-talk and the language of other people. Listen to what they say when things go badly and when things go well. Guide people to have a more positive explanatory style and encourage and use this language with those people around you to keep everybody in an optimistic frame of mind.

Control your focus.

A large part of the way we feel is driven by our sense of control. Being in control gives us comfort and reassurance in situations, especially new ones. The feeling of security this gives us is a very powerful one indeed. When we lack it we can feel stressed, anxious, and uneasy, which is obviously detrimental to our performance.

But could this feeling be powerful enough to influence our own death?

In the late 1970's, Ellen Langer was researching the power of this perceived sense of control. In one classic experiment, residents of a nursing home were given a plant to look after. A group of other residents were also given an identical plant, but were told that the nursing staff would look after it. Six months later, the residents who had been deprived of even this small sense of control were significantly less happy, healthy, and active than the other group.

Even more tragically, 30 percent of the residents who had not been given a plant to look after had died, while only 15 percent of the group given control over the plant had passed away.

The feeling of control is so powerful, we often seek to convince ourselves that we have control over things we actually don't. In sport, the use of superstitions calms this need for a sense of control. Some athletes put their kit on in a certain order because they think it will make them play better, or wear "lucky" items to help them feel in control of the situation.

It is important that people feel calm and confident to perform at a high level. Therefore, helping them achieve a sense of control is key.

This all ties back in with the work of Edward Deci and his Self-Determination Theory, where he states that people have three innate psychological needs that require fulfilling for optimal performance and motivation. One of those is a need for autonomy—having a sense of control over our own lives, the need to feel we have choices.

Think about how you can increase this sense of control for people by giving them more autonomy.

In what areas can you give people more ownership over what they do?

What could you delegate more of?

Create an environment that gives people more autonomy and a sense of control over what they are doing. By doing so, you will engage them at a deeper level and drive higher performance.

"Control the controllable."

Think of a situation that is causing you or your team some stress and concern. Draw two circles like the ones below and then list all the things within your control in the inner circle, and all of the things outside of your control in the outer circle. Then, make a list of all the things you can do something about in the inner circle, and let go of the rest.

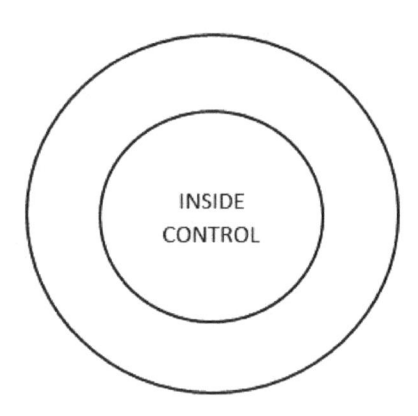

INSIDE CONTROL

Response-ability.

Controlling your responses to the events that occur in your life has a huge influence over your results. The earlier example of the US swimmer Matt Biondi perfectly demonstrates the power of this. Sometimes results don't go to plan, like they didn't for Biondi in his first two races.

Many of the events that cause people stress, disappointment, and frustration can often be found outside of their control. Yet we fool ourselves into a perceived sense of control over many events because it gives us a sense of security.

One of the few things we really do have control over is the way we think and the way we behave—our response-ability (ability to respond to events).

Great leaders control what they can control and don't waste much time worrying about the rest. When you are totally focused on what you can control, you will feel calmer and more focused, and be much more effective. This goes for all those around you too—make sure you and your team are fully focused on doing the things you can control.

The story on the following page illustrates the power of response-ability.

In 1990, a girl called Joanne responded to an advertisement in a national newspaper to teach English to children in Portugal. Whilst out there, she met a man, got married, and had a child. Sadly, her marriage only lasted thirteen months.

Joanne moved to Edinburgh, where her younger sister lived. She felt like the biggest failure she knew at the time. Her marriage had broken down and she was jobless with a dependent child. She was diagnosed with clinical depression, and had even contemplated suicide. With her situation desperate, she signed up for welfare benefits.

Whilst studying for her PGCE (so she could become a teacher in Scotland), Joanne worked on a book idea she had been harbouring for a couple of years. At night, whilst trying to get her daughter to sleep, she would rock up at her local café and write.

She finished the manuscript, written on an old typewriter, in 1995, and was connected to a literary agent who agreed to represent her in the search for a publisher. She was rejected by twelve publishing houses. The chairman of the thirteenth publishing house gave the first chapter to his daughter, who, upon reading it, demanded that he publish her book. Joanne received a £1,500 advance to finish the book, but was told by the same chairman to get herself a day job as she "probably won't make that much money from selling books".

Bloomsbury, the publishing house, printed 1,000 copies of Joanne's first book. It went on to win several awards and inspired Joanne to write several more award-winning novels. Her last four efforts have consecutively set records as the fastest sellers in history and have been translated into 65 different languages.

As for "probably won't make that much money from selling books"? Her first three combined made £350 million!

You may have guessed by now that I am talking about Joanne Rowling (JK Rowling), the author of the Harry Potter books.

The lesson?

It's not the events of your life that define you, but your response to those events. Make sure you stay focused on all the things you can control and respond in the best possible fashion.

Use the space below to list some of the challenges you are facing at the moment. Consider what is inside your control and what is not and then what action you will take as a result.

Rewiring.

Try the following exercises to rewire your brain for smarter, more productive and optimistic thinking:

1. For thirty days, start each day by listing three things you are grateful for or looking forward to that day, and end the day listing five things that went well and one thing to improve.

    Review how you feel after the thirty days and whether you can notice a difference in the way you feel.

2. Challenge your ANTs—Automatic Negative Thoughts. We all have reoccurring negative thoughts that pop into our minds, and if left to their own devices, they can grow and grow and seriously hinder our performance.

    Make a list of the events that you are thinking negatively around and next to each event, create two columns marked ANTs (Automatic Negative Thoughts) and NPT (New Positive Thoughts). For each negative thought, create a new empowering thought to think instead, and practise thinking the new thoughts on a daily basis. If it helps, look at your list daily.

3. Practise positive recall to train your brain to remember the positives and develop greater feelings of confidence in your abilities.

    List 5–7 achievements and a description under each of these headings:

Result Achieved | How It Made You Feel | Inner Commentary |

Keep these in a journal or somewhere you will see them often, reminding you and your brain of how it felt to succeed. Recall these events daily.

You could even create a "success jar", writing down the above details on a piece of paper every time you achieve something and placing it in a jar. At the end of the year, you will have a jar full of positive memories from that year.

Make it Happen.

"My powers are ordinary. Only my application brings me success."

Isaac Newton

We have covered a lot of ground in this book so far, looking at many interesting concepts, theories, and scientific studies which demonstrate the challenge of high performance and effective leadership.

The theories and the science may be interesting, but they are of no use to us unless we can put into practice what we have learnt. In this final chapter, we will look at how you can do that more effectively.

Simplicity is the ultimate sophistication.

Steve Jobs started Apple in 1976 in his parents' garage. He was ousted from the company in 1985, returned to rescue it from the verge of bankruptcy in 1997, and built it into the world's most valuable company by the time he died in 2011.

Jobs placed a huge emphasis on simplifying things and eliminating the unnecessary. This was one of Jobs' key strengths, and partly how he managed to take Apple to the heights of success and world domination. He was relentlessly focused on simplifying Apple's products to make them not only more user friendly, but also more elegant and stylish.

During the design of the iPod interface, Jobs continuously tried to find ways to reduce clutter. He insisted on being able to get to whatever he wanted in three clicks. One navigation screen, for example, asked users whether they wanted to search by song, album, or artist. Jobs challenged the designers on why that screen was necessary. After much consideration, they scrapped it.

Tony Fadell, who lead the iPod team, said, "There would be times when we'd rack our brains on a user interface problem, and he would go, 'Did you think of this?' And then we'd all go, 'Holy shit.' He'd redefine the problem or approach, and our little problem would go away."

Jobs simplified the design to such an extent that he challenged the need for the on/off button. The team were defensive at first, but later realised it wasn't essential. Jobs was helping everybody to look at things differently and challenge convention. They built the device to gradually power down if it wasn't being used and reawaken when it was. Simple.

> "If you can't explain it to a six-year-old, you don't understand it yourself."
>
> **Einstein**

The power of simplicity is not just to be restricted to the use of product design and ideas, however. The use of simplicity is valid in every domain of what you do as a leader, from the way you communicate and give instructions, to the actions and ideas you implement yourself.

Clive Woodward and the England Rugby team utilised this simplicity in determining their purpose for winning the Rugby World Cup—to inspire the nation. Simple.

No full-page documents with fancy straplines and corporate jargon. Simple, emotive language that people can understand. Three words too.

Keeping in line with this idea of simplicity, I have condensed the key concepts and strategies discussed so far in this book into twenty-five take-away ideas, broken down into five blocks of five:

1. We often assume others will take the lead. Look for opportunities to take the initiative instead of being a "bystander".
2. We make assumptions. We miss obvious details. We make poor judgements. Many of our problems arise from the same level of thinking we've always had. Practise challenging assumptions and thinking outside of the box.
3. Embrace new ideas and create a culture where any idea is a good idea, otherwise people will fail to offer them. Don't limit others. Remove the fear for them to express their creativity.
4. We often see what we expect to see and find what we expect to find. Learn to challenge your expectations.
5. Innovation and advancement begin with leaps in thinking. Challenge the norm.

6. Reframe failure. Create a culture where people are not scorned for failing, but failing to try.
7. Change starts with ourselves. Challenge your own perceptions and expectations first. When we change the way we look at things, the things we look at change.
8. Adopt a growth mindset. Never stop trying to become qualified for the job.
9. Be humble enough to spot new opportunities in every situation. Don't let your own self-importance prevent you from improving even further as a leader.
10. True self-confidence allows us to be open, welcome change, and embrace new ideas, regardless of their source.

11. Create an environment where people thrive on challenge and growth. Place an emphasis on learning and not just on end results. Continued growth will bring continued results.
12. Nothing is impossible and it's rarely too late—remember Carly?
13. Be careful what you expect of others. You are more influential than you think. See the best in people, even when they cannot see it in themselves.
14. We are emotional creatures. We are driven by emotion first, reason second. Engage people at an emotional level. Reason leads to conclusion, emotion leads to action.
15. The best leaders and the best teams start with "why". Get people focused on the purpose of what you are doing. If you want to move people, then learn to communicate with heart like Martin Luther King.

16. The most effective motivation is intrinsic. The zone is where your best work is produced. Give people work that provides them with the optimal challenge and you will see the best out of them.
17. Be the inspirational change and lead the way by practicing the ABC Formula.
18. It's easy to notice all the things that have gone wrong. Focus your attention on what goes well more often. Concentrate on success to replicate it. Energy flows where focus goes.
19. Offer genuine praise and feedback when you notice people applying themselves. Praising effort over results will result in more growth mindsets.
20. Rewards often work in the short term, but if you want lasting motivation, focus on making the job more enjoyable.

21. Create an environment where people can flourish. Give them challenges that match their skill level. Provide opportunities for people to learn and develop. Help people to see the difference they make.
22. Make sure you are creating a good impression. Start every interaction with the right attitude. The first four minutes are crucial.
23. When your thinking fails you, act your way into a positive emotional state. Body language is the largest part of your communication.
24. Stay enthused by using optimistic language. Listen out for other people's language to predict where they are on the optimism scale.
25. Give people a sense of autonomy and control over what they do and you will engage them at a deeper level. Focus all your attention on the controllable and let go of the rest.

Before you start planning on putting them all into practice, let me share another idea with you first.

Less is more.

In 1997, when Steve Jobs returned to Apple, they were producing lots of different versions of the Macintosh computer. They had lots of products and versions and Jobs found it far too confusing. After weeks of product reviews and brainstorming sessions, Jobs had heard enough. One day, he grabbed a pen and made his way to a whiteboard, where he drew a grid of four squares.

At the top of the grid, above each column, he wrote "Consumer" and "Pro". Down the sides of the grid he wrote "Desktop" and "Portable". He told his colleagues there and then that they were going to focus on four great products, one in each quadrant. Everything else? Cancelled.

The room was stunned to silence.

"Is he crazy? Does he know how much time has gone into those products?"

Jobs got Apple focused on making just four computers, and by doing so, he saved the company. Jobs understood that execution is often about eliminating the distractions and the unnecessary.

"Deciding what not to do is as important as deciding what to do," said Jobs. "It's true for companies and it's true for products."

Once Jobs got the company focused again and back into a strong position, he started taking his top 100 people away on a retreat each year. On the last day of the retreat, he would stand in front of a whiteboard and ask, "What are the 10 things we should be doing next?". People would be doing their utmost to have their suggestions on the list, with Jobs policing the ideas and writing down the ones which he approved of. After lots of discussion and strict elimination, the group would get the list down to just ten ideas. Then Jobs would take his pen and cross out seven of them and announce, "We can only do three."

Towards the end of Steve Jobs' life, he was visited by Larry Page, who co-founded Google and was about to take control over the company again. At the time, the companies were feuding, but Jobs was still willing to share some advice with Page.

"The main thing I stressed was focus," said Jobs.

He told him to get focused on no more than five products and drop the rest, because the rest will drag you down. Jobs explained that the more products they try to master, the lesser quality each of them will be. Few of them will be great. Page took Jobs' advice and honed the company's focus on a few key products.

Jobs believed that it is much better to be great at a few things, rather than simply good at lots. His time spent in India, and practising Zen Buddhism and meditation, taught him the value of singular focus, and when he adopted this approach with Apple, he transformed the company and put his dent in the universe.

Why is it difficult to exert this kind of focus and why don't more people do it?

Barry Schwartz, a psychologist and author of the book *The Paradox of Choice*, explains how too much choice not only leaves people less likely to make a decision, but also dissatisfied with the decisions they do make.

In one study, researchers set up two displays of jam at a gourmet food store for customers to try samples. They offered them a coupon for a discount if they bought a jar. In one display there were six jams, and in the other, twenty-four. Thirty percent of people exposed to the smaller selection bought a jar of jam, but only three percent of those exposed to the larger selection did.

When Dave Lewis took over at Tesco in 2015, he was determined to make the shopping experience easier in his stores by reducing the often confusing range of choice. He reduced the product range down by a third, from 90,000 products to 60,000 products. This was, in part, a response to the growing competition coming from Aldi and Lidl, whose market share had been continuously growing while they only offer between 2,000 and 3,000 product lines.

For example, Tesco used to offer twenty-eight different types of tomato ketchup, while in Aldi there was just one, available in one size only. Simple. Tesco also offered 224 kinds of air freshener, while Aldi only offered 12. Choosing from 12 would give me a headache, never mind 224!

Decision fatigue.

Psychological research shows that self-control and willpower draw upon a limited resource of mental energy, and this can affect our ability to make decisions.

Psychologist Roy Baumeister and his colleagues have researched this area heavily, finding that efforts of will and self-control are tiring. They showed that people who initially resisted the temptation of chocolates were subsequently less able to persist on a difficult and frustrating puzzle task. They also demonstrated that when people voluntarily gave a speech that included beliefs contrary to their own, they were also less able to persist on the difficult puzzle.

They termed this effect "ego depletion".

The evidence is fairly persuasive. When we have to exert self-control in one task, we feel less like making the effort in another. Hence the reason productivity leaders advise us to start the day with our most difficult or important tasks.

"You'll see I wear only grey or blue suits. I'm trying to pare down decisions. I don't want to make decisions about what I'm eating or wearing, because I have too many other decisions to make."

Barack Obama clearly understood the need for minimising ego depletion.

Use this knowledge to maximise your application of the strategies covered in this book. Go back to the twenty-five take-away ideas and apply the Steve Jobs rule of three to it.

What are the top three ideas that will make the biggest difference to your efforts as a leader right now?

Focus on mastering those first.

If you need some help deciding on which of the lessons to apply, consider the discovery of the Italian economist Vilfredo Pareto.

In 1906, Pareto made an interesting observation about the spread of wealth across Italy. He noticed that 80 percent of the land was owned by 20 percent of the population. He then noticed the same pattern in his garden, of all places, observing that 20 percent of the peapods contained 80 percent of the peas. This pattern, showing that the distribution of things in life is not spread evenly, was named after Pareto as "the Pareto Principle". The pattern has many applications to multiple scenarios, however the basic premise is that in most situations, there are a few vital causes of the overall result.

In any given task, for example, 20 percent of the actions you take will likely generate about 80 percent of the results you produce.

Identify your vital few lessons and ideas you have discovered from this book and get to work on applying them. This is just one of the few ways that great leaders make it happen. They know they cannot do everything, so they make sure the actions they do take have the greatest possible impact—Steve Jobs' relentless desire to eliminate products and ideas is a great example of this.

Remember the lesson "less is more".

And if it is simply too ego depleting for you to decide, then just start at the top of the list and spend two weeks on each idea, meaning that in twelve months' time you will have applied all of the key lessons in this book.

The Deadly P.

You have probably heard the term. It's been doing the rounds now for a few years—procrastination. The act of delaying what you should be doing in favour of something easier and less meaningful.

We all do it. Great at it we are too!

Being somebody who makes it happen is about putting into practice the things that you know make a difference. It would be a great waste of time to read this book and not use any of the ideas contained within it. But if we leave that to chance, you can put your money on that happening.

Dan Ariely, a professor of psychology and economics, has done some interesting research in this area. Ariely noticed that procrastination is something very prevalent with his students. I'm sure you can recall leaving assignments and projects to the very last minute plenty of times, just like Dan noticed with his students.

He decided to run an experiment to examine what was going on. He gave his students the choice of when to set the deadline for three assignments they had been given. The condition was that once they chose a date, they must stick with that date or they would receive a penalty for a late submission.

Rational thinking would tell us that the more time you have to work on something, the better the work will be. Thus, it would be in the interest of the students to choose the very last date available to hand their work in. Interestingly, Ariely found that most students decided to spread their deadlines out across the semester, showing they were aware of their tendency to give in to procrastination the more time they had.

To test this further, he gave a second class rigid deadlines on the fourth, eighth, and twelfth week. A third class was also told that they could submit their work at the end of the semester.

When he compared the results of all the groups, he found that the students with rigid deadlines performed the best and the ones with all the deadlines at the end did the worst. The students who got to choose their deadlines were in the middle. The results showed the tendency for students to procrastinate on their work, affecting the quality of it, and that restricting their freedom produced better results.

Deadlines work. They create a sense of urgency, which in turn gives people a greater sense of accomplishment and self-esteem when they get things done. Accountability is a key part of this too, so perhaps you could partner with somebody and hold each other accountable to your take-away actions and ideas.

Getting the best out of people is a balance between giving them freedom and autonomy but also making sure they have a clear deadline for when they must produce.

A letter worth a fortune.

We are approaching the end of the book now and I hope you are eager to put the book down and start making it happen.

Whilst you may have had several big picture ideas throughout this book, what matters now is the smaller daily disciplines of putting these ideas into action. This is something that the famous banker JP Morgan was cleverly reminded of one evening after leaving his office.

A young man holding an envelope in his hand approached Mr Morgan and said, "Sir, in my hand I hold a guaranteed formula for success which I will gladly sell to you for twenty-five thousand dollars."

Morgan was smart enough to trial the formula on the promise that if he liked it, then he would pay the man his asking price.

Several days later Morgan met up with the gentleman and handed over a cheque for $25,000.

Inside the envelope was a piece of paper which read:

1. Every morning, write a list of the things that need to be done that day.
2. Do them.

As you put this book down, please remember the lesson from this story and make sure that each day, you are putting things on your list that are going to make the difference.

Most importantly: do them, and be a leader who makes it happen.

Research shows that committing our actions to paper increases the chances of follow through. Use the chart below to increase your chances of success.

Actions I will now take   **By when**

Closing Comments

I hope you enjoyed reading my book and I really appreciate the time you have invested. Now it is over to you to implement the ideas that have resonated with you.

If you did enjoy the read, then please spread the word to your friends, colleagues and loved ones who you think it would also interest. But don't lend them your copy, buy them one instead and then we all benefit!

If you want to get in touch with me then please check out the details below.

All my best,

Martin.

Getting in Touch

Should you wish to get in touch to share how this book has helped you, or you would like to enquire about working with Martin and having him share the messages in this book in one of his highly engaging talks, please get in touch at the following address:

contact@martinroberthall.co.uk

or visit www.martinroberthall.co.uk

Acknowledgements

I would like to thank all the people that have made this book possible for me, the many friends and family who have made it possible and always supported my work. You know who you are.

I would also like to say thank you to Publish Nation for their patience and guidance in helping me get this over the line!

I would like to thank the team at Nothing But Epic for their fantastic design work on my branding, in particular Craig and Ben.

Most of all I would like to thank you the reader and all of my clients for investing your time and money in my work. You make it possible and you are the reason why I do it, without you I wouldn't have a business and be able to express my passion through my writing and speaking.

I will continue to learn and bring you the best of my knowledge.

Bibliography

Ariely, D. (2008). Predictably Irrational. The Hidden Forces that Shape Our Decisions. Harper Collins.

Ciadini, R. (2007). Influence: The Psychology of Persuasion. Harper Business Rev.

Collins, J & Porras, J. (1994). Built to Last: Successful Habits of Visionary Companies. Harper Business.

Collins, J. (2001). Good to great: Why some companies make the leap ... and others don't. New York, NY: Harper Business.

Darley, J. M. & Latané, B. (1968). "Bystander intervention in emergencies: Diffusion of responsibility". Journal of Personality and Social Psychology. 8: 377–383

Darley, J. M., & Latané, B. (1970). The unresponsive bystander: why doesn't he help? New York, NY: Appleton Century Crofts.

Deci, E. L. (1971). "Effects of externally mediated rewards on intrinsic motivation". Journal of Personality and Social Psychology. 18: 105–115

Deci, E. (1997) Why We Do What We Do: Understanding Self-Motivation. Penguin Books.

Dweck, C. S. (2006). Mindset: The new psychology of success. New York: Random House.

https://www.theguardian.com/lifeandstyle/2015/oct/21/choice-stressing-us-out-dating-partners-monopolies - Stuart Jeffries - Why too much choice is stressing us out.

Isaacson, W. (2009) Steve Jobs: The Exclusive Biography. Little Brown, London.

Kahneman, D. (2011). Thinking, fast and slow. New York: Farrar, Straus and Giroux.

Laird, J. (2007). Feelings: The Perception of Self. Oxford University Press.

Latane, B. & Rodin, J. (1969) A lady in distress: Inhibiting effects of friends and strangers on bystander intervention. Journal of Experimental Social Psychology, 5(2), 189-202.

Lepper, Mark R.; Greene, David; Nisbett, Richard E. "Undermining children's intrinsic interest with extrinsic reward: A test of the "overjustification" hypothesis". Journal of Personality and Social Psychology, Vol 28(1), Oct 1973, 129-137.

Pink, Daniel H. 2009. Drive: the surprising truth about what motivates us. New York, NY: Riverhead Books.

Rosenthal, R.; Jacobson, L. (1968). Pygmalion in the Classroom. New York: Holt, Rinehart & Winston.

Rosenthal, Robert; Jacobson, Lenore (1992). Pygmalion in the classroom (Expanded ed.). New York: Irvington.

Sinek, S. (2011). Start With Why: How Great Leaders Inspire Everyone To Take Action. Penguin.

Vallerand, R. J.; Reid, G. (1984). "On the causal effects of perceived competence on intrinsic motivation: A test of cognitive evaluation theory". Journal of Sport Psychology. 6: 94–102

Welch, J. (2003). Straight from the Gut. Grand Central Publishing.

Woodward, C. (2005). Winning! Hodder Paperbacks.

Notes

Notes

"You can't build a reputation on what you are going to do."

Henry Ford